A Ghost Hunter's Guide to The Most Haunted Historic Sites In America

Terrance Zepke

Terrance Zepke

WHAT REVIEWERS ARE SAYING ABOUT ZEPKE'S MOST HAUNTED SERIES

"One of the things I really like about Terrance's book is that it is such an easy read. The tidbits of history keep you turning the pages, and you also learn about the paranormal investigators, who have used a variety of paranormal investigation tools…*A Ghost Hunter's Guide To The Most Haunted Places in America* is one of those books that keeps your imagination wondering what really happened."
-Josh Schubert, **USA Travel Magazine**

"…*A Ghost Hunter's Guide To The Most Haunted Places in America*" explores the story behind these ghost story settings all throughout the country, from theaters, old factories, asylums, homes prisons, and much more. A Ghost Hunter's Guide to The Most Haunted Places in America is a must for lovers of the paranormal in America. Highly recommended.
-James A. Cox, **Midwest Book Review**

"…while the words "adventure travel" may conjure up images of the remote or the foreign, a new book suggests that some wild rides are much closer to home. Zepke documents the supernatural in *A Ghost Hunter's Guide to the Most Haunted Houses in America*. As she points out, "Who else but an adventurous and brave soul would dare to spend time in a haunted dwelling—and pay good money to do so?"
–Sarah Robbins, **Publishers Weekly**

"From a lunatic asylum to a brewery, ghostly presences inhabit all these places. Complete directions and site information is provided. Even if you don't get a chance to visit each of these locations, the stories and the black-and-white photos are fascinating.
-Marcella Gauthier, **Escapees Magazine**

If you like the paranormal, you'll love this book…I like how the author gives the history of each place, helping me to understand the why of the hauntings. The fun facts were enlightening. I like that the addresses and websites were included, making it simpler to do more research, or in my case, checking on availability. I'm a sucker for a good scare.
-Julie Baswell (**Amazon Reader Review**)

A Ghost Hunter's Guide to the Most Haunted Historic Sites in America

"…From Georgia to California, Terrance writes about places that are home to a ghost or two -- and tells the horrible tales that led to these creatures remaining close to where they died. Her first chapter is about the Trans-Allegheny Lunatic Asylum in West Virginia, the place that creeped her out the most in her investigations into the paranormal -- and the one closest to where I live. It is told that many of the poor souls who died in the facility -- often from experimental treatments and procedures -- continue to roam the halls. Yawsa."
-Teresa Flatley, **BoomThis! Magazine**

"You don't have to believe in ghosts to realize that certain places in our national history are haunted with legends and spirits of long ago. Terrance Zepke grew up in South Carolina knowing the tales of colonial pirates, Civil War legends, the impact of lowcountry voodoo, and the famous residents of weathered cemeteries…places you probably best not visit at night, She's written books such as *Coastal South Carolina: Welcome to the Lowcountry, Best Ghost Tales of South Carolina, Pirates of the Carolinas*, and her latest book, *A Ghost Hunter's Guide to the Most Haunted Places in America*, investigates saloons and cemeteries, former sanitariums, and penitentiaries across America where rumors of strange phenomenon seem to have some bearing…Terrance is one of the most schooled experts on the paranormal in the United States."
–Rick Steves, **Travel with Rick Steves**

"…Zepke herself has always loved a good ghost story and heard many as she was growing up in the Carolinas. Now she has many books recording not only the stories she loves but also the history and photos of the places named. These places have all been investigated and proven haunted by the most sophisticated modern scientific equipment such as EMF detectors, which register electrical and magnetic fields, and EVP's (Electronic Voice Phenomenon), which digitally records sounds the human ear cannot detect. Each place Zepke writes about has all the tour contact information also and many black and white photos. A fun way to plan a trip, if you aren't afraid!"
-Bonny Neely (**Top 1,000 Amazon Reviewer**)

Terrance Zepke

This book was full of so many great facts and figures as well as photos of some truly scary looking places. While I have not visited any of these places, after reading this I am more apt to seek them out, especially with a daughter that loves scary things. The book was well written, short and to the point, but the author does not leave out any detail. Zepke does a great job at describing the locations completely and gives you as a reader a clear glimpse into what you can expect (or not expect) when you visit these locations. It was well written and for anyone who loves haunted places, this is definitely the book for you!
 -Dad of Divas **(Top 500 Amazon Reviewer)**

This book gave me goosebumps all over. It accurately describes places in real life that are haunted by ghosts and even tells you a bit about the ghosts themselves…The scariest thing about this book is you can actually visit these locations. If you want to see some ghosts on vacation, then this book is a must have in the planning stages. It will tell you where to go and what to look out for when you get there. My only suggestion is to be careful, a lot of the events around these ghosts are historical facts which may send more than just a chill down your spine.   **-Amazon Reader Review**

"…a journalist by training, she [Zepke] takes you on a tour of the Trans-Allegheny Lunatic Asylum in West Virginia, the Birdcage Theatre in Arizona, and the Colonial Park Cemetery in Georgia, among a dozen other places…"
 -Alan Caruba, **Bookviews.com** (National Book Critics Circle)

A Ghost Hunter's Guide to the Most Haunted Historic Sites in America

Copyright ©2016 by Terrance Zepke

All rights reserved. No part of this book shall be reproduced or transmitted in any form or by any means, electronic, mechanical, magnetic, and photographic including photocopying, recording or by any information storage and retrieval system, without prior written permission of the publisher. No patent liability is assumed with respect to the use of the information contained herein. Although every precaution has been taken in the preparation of this book, the publisher and author assume no responsibility for errors or omissions. Neither is any liability assumed for damages resulting from the use of the information contained herein.

ISBN-10: 1942738072
ISBN-13: 978-1-942738-07-7

Cover design by Michael Swing.

Safari Publishing

Inquiries should be addressed to: www.safaripublishing.net
For more about the author: www.terrancezepke.com

1.Ghosts. 2. Paranormal. 3. Hauntings-America. 4. American Folklore-Ghosts. 5. Ghost Investigations/Tours. 6. Haunted Historic Sites. I. Title.

Second Edition
Printed in the U.S.A.

Terrance Zepke

A Ghost Hunter's Guide to the Most Haunted Historic Sites in America

Introduction, 8

Hart Island, A.K.A. "Island of the Dead" (New York), 10
Gettysburg (Pennsylvania), 17
Alamo (Texas), 25
White House (Washington, D.C.), 32
Battleship North Carolina (North Carolina), 41
Alcatraz (California), 48
Statue of Liberty and Ellis Island (New York), 58
Mammoth Cave (Kentucky), 66
Harpers Ferry National Park (Virginia), 74
Grand Canyon (Arizona), 82
Empire State Building (New York), 91
Golden Gate Bridge (California), 98
Wrigley Field (Illinois), 105
King's Arms Tavern (Virginia), 112
Hollywood Sign (California), 118

Resources, 127
Fun Quiz, 130
Titles by Terrance, 133
Sneak Peak, 150
Index, 157

A Ghost Hunter's Guide to the Most Haunted Historic Sites in America

About the Author

Terrance Zepke loves ghost stories and travel. She has lived and traveled all over the world during her career as a freelance adventure travel writer. She has explored every continent and enjoyed all kinds of adventures—from dog-sledding in the Arctic to surviving an overnight stay in a very haunted lunatic asylum. Even though she has lived in exciting cities, such as Honolulu and London, she calls the Carolinas her "true home." She can't decide which state she likes best so she divides her time between North and South Carolina. She grew up in the South Carolina Lowcountry, which is what ignited her interest in ghosts. The Lowcountry is full of haunted places and tales of boo hags, hoodoo, and haints. Terrance has written numerous books on the history and folklore of the Carolinas, as well as dozens of travel guides (See the back of this book for a list of all titles).

Introduction

    I love history. I can lose all track of time exploring historic sites, especially if they are haunted too. You better believe that I loved every minute I spent researching this book. After a great deal of research, I have compiled this list of the most haunted historic sites in America. If you like this book, be sure to read other books in this series, such as *A Ghost Hunter's Guide to the Most Haunted Houses in America* and *A Ghost Hunter's Guide to the Most Haunted Hotels & Inns in America.*

    If you're a history buff like me, you will appreciate learning more about some of our greatest national treasures, including who haunts them and why. I learned a lot while writing this book. For example, I discovered Hart Island. I never even knew this utterly creepy place existed. If you don't know about this spooky little island (a.k.a. "Island of the Dead")—or know very little about it—this book will reveal its gruesome and haunted history.

    Learn all about Mammoth Cave. Did you know that it's the largest cave in the world? What a fabulously frightening place it is! This cave plays a remarkable role in our nation's history and park system—and is home to a few ghosts too.

    Read on to find out all about the most haunted baseball stadium in America, which is home to a trio of ghosts, and you'll also learn about The Curse of Billy Goat.

    Discover what the Empire State Building, Golden Gate Bridge, and the Hollywood Sign have in common. It should be no surprise that it is a spooky and sinister connection.

    Learn all about the ghosts, including a former president who is still in residence, who have been seen and heard throughout the White House by hundreds of credible witnesses.

    My favorite chapters in *A Ghost Hunter's Guide to the Most Haunted Historic Sites in America* are The Alamo, Alcatraz, and *Battleship NC*. The reason being that I really enjoyed exploring these places most of all. It is interesting to try to imagine what they must have been like when they were inhabited.

    Most of the sites discussed in this reference are iconic symbols.

They signify what makes our nation great by reminding us of our past and our forefathers—of the battles we have fought for freedom and liberty. They represent our ideals and values. They reveal our hopes and dreams.

And these places are haunted by the spirits of men and women who play an important role in the history—and the popularity—of these special places. And all the sites discussed in this book are open to the public, except Hart Island. So you can visit and explore to your heart's content and maybe even have a ghostly encounter.

At the end of each chapter, there is detailed visitor information, including tour options, special seasonal events, accessibility, tourist tips, directions, and more. Learn everything you need to know before you go, including the best time to visit and other important visitor information.

If you would like to download free ghost and travel reports or get *MostlyGhostly* updates, visit www.terrancezepke.com. If you'd like to learn more about how to travel cheap and listen to my *Über Adventures* podcast, visit www.terrancetalkstravel.com.

Terrance Zepke

Hart Island

Hart Island

A trench at the potter's field on Hart Island, circa 1890 by **Jacob Riis**

FUN FACTS:

The island has served as home to many different enterprises and institutions through the years.

It is one of the most mysterious places in America—and haunted too!

Talk about scary; its nickname is ISLAND OF THE DEAD.

The History

What a dark and complex history this place has. It seems like it was a host to all kinds of horrible things over the years. While it may not be officially recognized as a historic site, it has great historical significance. Thousands of Confederate soldiers captured during the Civil War were imprisoned here. 3,413 men were imprisoned here with 235 of them dying while being held in this prisoner of war camp. These men were buried in Soldier's Plot on Hart Island.

The first woman buried on Hart Island was twenty-four-year-old Louisa Van Slyke in 1869. The oldest person buried here is Ruth Proskauer Smith, who died in 2010 at the ripe old age of 102.

When the yellow fever epidemic struck New York in 1870, the island became a quarantine station. An asylum for women was established in 1885. The United States Navy used the island as a military prison during WWII. Servicemen who were found guilty of military misconduct were sent here to serve their time. At one point, nearly 3,000 Navy, Marine, and Coast Guard personnel were incarcerated here.

The island hosted a drug rehabilitation center and a TB sanitarium. And the island was home to the Nike missile base. There was even a ball field on the island for a while. Boys and young men who were sent to the Reformatory for Misdemeanants workhouse on the island played the men stationed at the missile battery on Kratter Field. Not long after that, the reformatory was closed and so was the missile base. The reformatory closed due to misconduct. The boys were being abused and tortured by their supervisors.

For a brief time, an all-black amusement park operated on the south tip of the island. Known as the Negro Coney Island, the rides, pavilion, and boardwalk overlooked hundreds of graves and the reformatory school.

By the early 1900s, Hart Island had become one giant burial ground. Anyone in the great New York City area who could not afford a proper burial or who wasn't promptly claimed by family members were buried in mass graves on the island. Until 2007, a New York law stipulated that relatives had only forty-eight hours to claim a body. If it was not claimed by that time, the government released the body to a medical school or a mortuary school. If for whatever reason, those institutions didn't want the corpse, it was sent to Hart Island.

Hart Island is owned by New York City and operated by the New York Department of Corrections. The men, women, and children who are still being laid to rest on Hart Island are being buried by Rikers Island inmates. It is the largest tax-funded cemetery in the world. It is standard practice to bury the adults three coffins deep and two coffins across. Babies and children are stacked five deep and up to twenty across. Amputated body parts are also disposed of here. They are placed in pine boxes marked "limbs" and buried in some random among the other coffins.

Convalescent Hospital on Hart Island, 1877.

Sidebar: Scary nicknames include BIGGEST GRAVEYARD IN THE WORLD, NEW YORK CITY'S POTTER FIELD, and ISLAND OF THE DEAD.

The Hauntings

With more than one million people being unceremoniously buried in mass graves, it's no wonder this is one of the most haunted sites in the U.S. Most of these poor souls died alone, lonely, and homeless. Some died after suffering a long time from mental illness or physical afflictions. It seems that at least some of these spirits may not be able to rest in peace.

No official investigation has ever taken place on the island due to its strict security, so it is hard to speak with any certainty about paranormal activity. However, I feel certain that with this much tragic history and death, there is a lot of supernatural activity.

The sounds of boys screaming and crying in anguish have been reported by former hospital staff. It is believed these are the spirits of the reformatory boys who were badly tortured while here. Those that didn't die from the cruel abuse they were subjected to, probably died from the unsafe conditions. Contagious patients were put in the same ward as the boys. They were made to share personal items, such as razors and towels with the TB patients.

I cannot find an exact accounting of how many buildings still exist on the island. Including ruins, I believe there are at least three dozen structures. It is well- documented that there was a large hospital complex, reformatory school, and outbuildings, missile base, amusement park, and jail.

A Ghost Hunter's Guide to the Most Haunted Historic Sites in America

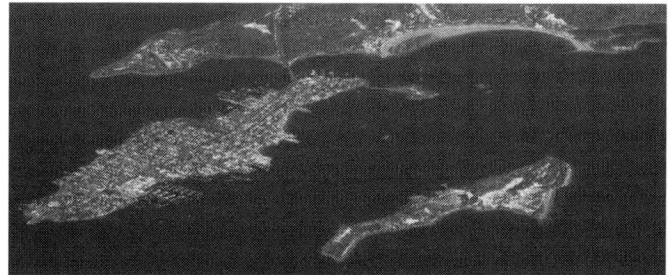

Hart Island is accessible only by boat.

Visitor Information

Hart Island is on the western end of Long Island Sound, next to the Bronx. No one is permitted on the one-mile-long by one-quarter-mile-wide island, except Rikers Island inmates, guards, and the deceased.

Trespassers will be prosecuted. The government is quite serious about their NO TRESPASSING policy. The only way one could get on the island is by private boat, but security is vigilant. A government ferry brings the prisoners over to the island.

To learn more about Hart Island visit https://www.hartisland.net/.

New York City is 7 hours from Cleveland, Ohio (461 miles); 12 hours from Augusta, GA (777 miles); and 4 hours from Boston, MA (214 miles).

A Ghost Hunter's Guide to the Most Haunted Historic Sites in America

Gettysburg

Gettysburg

FUN FACTS:

There are approximately 1,328 monuments, markers and memorials at Gettysburg National Military Park. There are several ways to explore the park, including a tour by a park ranger, commercial bus tour, and independently.

Only Union soldiers are buried in the Soldiers' National Cemetery at Gettysburg. Confederate soldiers were interred at Hollywood Cemetery in Richmond, Virginia before being returned to Georgia, Virginia, and the Carolinas from 1871 - 1873.

It is no wonder this place is haunted given that the Battle of Gettysburg ended with the highest number of casualties of the Civil War.

A Ghost Hunter's Guide to the Most Haunted Historic Sites in America

The History

One of the most important battles of the Civil War was the Battle of Gettysburg. It was fought July 1–3, 1863, in and around Gettysburg, Pennsylvania. And it happened by chance. Neither army knew the whereabouts of the other when they converged coincidentally on the town of Gettysburg as Lee moved north and Mead moved south.

The Battle of Gettysburg came right after General Lee's victory at Chancellorsville, Virginia. Lee's army was put to the test in what was to be the most significant skirmish of this war.

Initially, Federal troops were forced to retreat, and things were looking good for the Confederate army. On the second day of this battle, fighting was intense and prolonged. But there was no victory for either side. By the third day of battle, more than 12,000 Confederate soldiers took part in a legendary assault known as Pickett's Charge. The attack was not only unsuccessful; it resulted in heavy casualties for the Confederates. Lee was forced to retreat to Virginia. The Confederates had lost the Battle of Gettysburg, and this defeat ultimately cost them the war. It was considered the "High Water Mark of the Rebellion."

At the end of this bloody, three-day battle, both armies had suffered high casualties. Almost one-third of the participants of the Battle of Gettysburg died during it. In fact, it was the bloodiest battle of the Civil War with 51,000 killed, wounded, missing, or captured.

The Hauntings

When the battle ended, there were far more wounded and dead left behind than there were residents of Gettysburg. Blood, body parts, and debris were scattered everywhere. There wasn't enough room in the makeshift hospital, so the wounded were taken to private homes and treated as best as the families were able. Some could do no more than make the men as comfortable as possible as they lay dying.

Corpses were strewn about all over the place as the entire town had been a battlefield. This being the middle of summer, the stench soon became awful. It took weeks to bury all the deceased. Some never got a proper burial. Is it any wonder this is one of the most haunted places in America?

The most haunted part of the battlefield is Devil's Den. This is probably due to the heavy fighting (and casualties) that occurred happened here on the second day of the Battle of Gettysburg. Reportedly, some corpses were tossed into the deep crevices rather than given a proper burial. A Texan soldier has been seen by many visitors and rangers over the years. But according to legend, Devil's Den was haunted long before this battle.

Today, the National Park Service has established a designated area as a national historic site. In reality, all of Gettysburg was a battlefield. This explains why supernatural encounters extend beyond the perimeters of the Gettysburg National Military Park.

A Ghost Hunter's Guide to the Most Haunted Historic Sites in America

At the time of the war, the town of Gettysburg had a population of 2,400. There were two schools: Lutheran Theological Seminary and Pennsylvania College. A dormitory at Pennsylvania College (which is now Gettysburg College) is one of the most haunted places on the campus. That's because it was commandeered during battle as a field hospital for the Confederates and the cupola was used as a watch tower.

Sometimes at night, students and employees have seen what appears to be a soldier pacing inside the cupola. Campus police have often been notified when the shadowy figure is seen. They never find anyone when they investigate and no sign that the locked entrance to the cupola has been tampered with.

Lots of "surgeries" took place in the basement when the former dorm was used as a hospital. These surgeries began with the doctors trying to save an arm or leg from a bullet would but usually ended in an amputation. According to a popular story that I believe originated with Gettysburg ghost expert Mark Nesbitt, two employees of the school had a gruesome ghostly encounter one night. Pennsylvania Hall is now an administrative building. Two women employees had worked late one night. They were tired and ready to go home. They got into the elevator and pushed the main floor. Instead of stopping, the elevator kept going down. When it reached the basement, the doors opened and the women witnessed one of these gory amputations. They screamed and pushed buttons but the elevator did not move. They said the men were in uniform, like they were soldiers. One man, obviously the doctor, was wearing a white apron that had blood all over it. There was blood everywhere and screams of pain. Finally, the elevator responded to their commands and they were taken to the main floor. They reported what they had witnessed, but there was no hospital scene found during an investigation.

Many private residences are said to be haunted. These alleged hauntings are not surprising given that soldiers were carried into these homes either during the battle to shelter the wounded or afterward to recuperate or await death. The most haunted dwellings include George Weikert House, Hummelbaugh House, and Rose Farm. Unexplainable sounds are most commonly reported, but a ghostly apparition has been seen on occasion.

Additionally, Cashtown Inn, Jennie Wade House, and the Farnsworth House Inn are haunted. Jennie Wade was the only civilian casualty of the Battle of Gettysburg. She was killed when a musket ball smashed through her door, killing her instantly. Residents, realizing they could suffer the same fate, soon abandoned their homes. Visitors can see all the bullet holes that riddle the walls of Farnsworth House Inn. One of the rooms has been locked to prevent guests from entering. This room was where a couple of Confederate sharpshooters were positioned. It is believed one or both of these soldiers were injured or killed here. The spirit(s) haunt this room, as well as several other areas of the Farnsworth House Inn.

Some visitors have reported the faint smell of peppermint while in Gettysburg. Is this linked to paranormal activity? Perhaps. Reportedly, the stench was so bad from the decaying corpses that the only way women could tolerate going out was to douse or spray their handkerchiefs with peppermint. They held the scented linens up to their noses to offset the horrific odor.

I never smelled any peppermint but did have a weird experience. Late one night, we sneaked into the park. I do not recommend this as you can get arrested for trespassing if caught. I didn't realize that at that time! Thank goodness we weren't caught. It was eerily dark and quiet. We sat down and waited in silence for a while. While we were in the park, we heard soft cries and faint clomping noises like horses' hooves. The cries may have been nocturnal creatures or possibly something supernatural. As to the clomping sounds, they do have horseback tours during the day but not at night. It could have been a park ranger on a horse, but that explanation doesn't make sense because rangers don't patrol on horseback at night.

Some visitors have seen a soldier roaming around or a skirmish. At the time, the witnesses thought the men were NPS employees or re-enactment participants. The few who tried to approach the lone man watched in amazement as it disappeared. Others who mentioned the re-enactment were told there was no such event scheduled that particular day. A soldier on horseback is seen briefly on occasion before it disappears. The smell of gunfire, moans, screams, and shouts have been heard. Some folks claim their cameras and video recorders have malfunctioned for no good reason (always in the same spots) inside the park.

Author's Note: Don't bother asking NPS employees to share stories or information. They have been instructed to not talk about paranormal activity. In my experience in Gettysburg and other NPS sites, the park rangers are not helpful in this area. In fact, a ranger at Fort Pulaski in Georgia was rude to me when I asked him about possible paranormal activity.

Visitor Information

Gettysburg National Military Park

1195 Baltimore Pike

Gettysburg, PA 17325

www.nps.gov/gett

There is a visitor's center, bookstore, snack bar, and museum on site. There is no charge to explore the park or visitors center, but there is a fee for the museum. Admission includes a film titled "A New Birth of Freedom" and the Gettysburg Cyclorama, which is a dramatic depiction of the famous 'Pickett's Charge.' Most of the houses and buildings in the park are not open to the public. The historic site is open year round but hours vary seasonally. Tour options include self-guided, a park ranger program, or a guided tour. For help planning your Gettysburg trip, check out http://www.destinationgettysburg.com/index.asp. If you're interested in a ghost tour, visit http://www.destinationgettysburg.com/things-to-do/gettysburg-ghost-tours.asp. My favorite paranormal experience is the **Farnsworth House Ghost Walks & Mourning Theater**. I highly recommend this option for those seeking spooky fun! You can learn more at http://www.farnsworthhouseinn.com/ghost-tours.html.

Gettysburg is 2.5 hours from Philadelphia (140 miles); 7.5 hours from Cincinnati (453 miles), Ohio; and 15 hours from Tampa (984 miles). Florida.

A Ghost Hunter's Guide to the Most Haunted Historic Sites in America

The Alamo

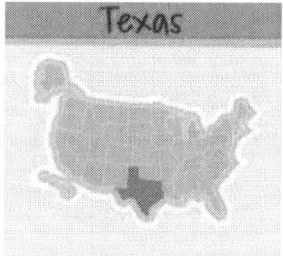

Terrance Zepke

The Alamo

FUN FACTS:

The first reported paranormal activity dates back to 1836.

The Alamo is the most popular tourist attraction in Texas.

There is reportedly a big treasure hidden somewhere at the Alamo, but if this is true, its location has not been discovered.

The History

Texas was once part of Spain and at that time was known as the Texas territory. By the early 1700s, the King of Spain sent Franciscan Friars to Texas to introduce Christianity to this territory. It was important to Spain's objective, which was to colonize America, that all natives and settlers be converted.

To this end, the friars set up missions all the way across Texas to the Rio Grande. One such mission was named the Alamo. In time, an eight-foot adobe and stone wall was erected around this church and its many outbuildings. This was done to safeguard the residents from Indian attacks.

By 1790, there were 275 men, women, and children living at the Alamo. Within a few years, Spanish soldiers were also present permanently at the Alamo to protect this civilian population. There was a real fear that someone else (like the U.S. or France), might try to lay claim to this vast land that some called "New Spain." Ultimately, Spain lost control of the Texas territory. They relinquished it to Mexico in 1821. The Mexican government allowed Anglo-Americans to establish colonies here as long as they recognized their subservience to Mexico.

But Sam Houston had other ideas. He believed that Texas should be independent of Mexico. And Sam Houston knew that was never going to happen as long as President and General Antonio Lopez de Santa Anna was alive and in charge Mexico and the Mexican Army.

In anticipation of conflict, Houston ordered the Alamo to be reinforced. The Battle of the Alamo is one of the most remarkable events in the history of our great nation. When Santa Anna heard what was happening at the Alamo, he got ready for a brief skirmish, which he anticipated would end in a total surrender. Instead, he got a thirteen-day battle that forever changed U.S. history.

While it may appear to be a big defeat for the U.S. due to all the loss of lives and ultimately the loss of control of the Alamo, it was anything but that. These brave men and women bought Sam Houston enough time to allow him to get the resources he needed to defeat the Mexican Army at the Battle of San Jacinto on April 21, 1836.

What gave the Battle of the Alamo its place in history was that 150 rebels held off more than 5,000 Mexican soldiers armed with twenty-one cannons and thousands of rifles for thirteen days—and caused 1,600 casualties to the Mexican Army!

The men who fought so valiantly at the Alamo, such as Jim Bowie, William Travis, and Davy Crockett, certainly earned their places in our history books.

Fall of the Alamo **by Robert Jenkins Oderdonk**

The Hauntings

There were so many casualties here between those who died during battle and those few survivors who were brutally executed by Santa Anna that it is no surprise that the Alamo is one of the most haunted places in America.

In addition to all the battle-related deaths, there was a cemetery here from 1724-1793. It is estimated that as many as 1,000 persons were buried in this graveyard. Bones and skulls are still being discovered by contractors.

The earliest ghostly activity dates back to a few weeks after the Battle of the Alamo. General Santa Anna sent men back to the Alamo to destroy it. Upon the arrival of his soldiers, six spirits appeared in the doorway warning the men not to go any farther. Some believe these were the spirits of the Franciscan Friars, while others believe they were the spirits of Bowie, Crockett, and some of the other heroes of the Battle of the Alamo. Whoever these spirits were they succeeded in scaring off the Mexican soldiers.

Santa Anna dispatched another group to destroy the Alamo. But when these soldiers arrived they saw a spirit up on the roof holding what appeared to be flaming balls of fire. These men quickly fled and refused to return. Santa Anna abandoned his plan to destroy the Alamo.

By the mid-1800s, the U.S. Army began repairing the abandoned Alamo. Strange events were reported by the workers. Reports of weird happenings continued throughout its history, including its time as a jail and police station for the City of San Antonio. Paranormal activity continues to be reported to this day.

Ghostly sentries have been spotted on the roof. Shadowy figures have been seen in the old barracks. Moaning and screaming have been heard, as well as the sounds of bugles, cannon fire, and horses galloping.

In the gardens next door, a cowboy specter is often been witnessed. A male spirit has been seen leaning out the front window of the old chapel, but he disappears as quickly as he appears. A female spirit has been seen at night on occasion near the old well. Is she one of the women who died during the Battle of the Alamo?

A Mexican soldier specter has been seen roaming the grounds. This may be the ghost of General Manuel Fernandez de Castrillon, who was sympathetic to the rebels. He promised the six survivors clemency, but Santa Anna murdered them all right in front of Castrillon.

And, of course, there have been Davy Crockett sightings. He has been seen by park rangers and visitors. A couple of boys have been seen following tour groups. Alamo defender, Anthony Wolfe, had his nine-year-old and twelve-year-old sons in the church. They were discovered by Mexican soldiers during the battle and subsequently killed. It is believed their young spirits still haunt the Alamo.

In fact, ghostly sightings have been reported on Alamo Plaza, as well as at the Alamo. Some of the rebels and Mexican soldiers were buried nearby in what is now a park and the Marriott Hotel. Paranormal activity has been reported in these places, as well. Now that the fortress walls have come down, perhaps these spirits roam more freely?

Some even believe that the ghost of John "Duke" Wayne is here. He filmed "The Alamo" and from that point on became obsessed with the battle and its dark history. After his death, visitors began reported sightings of a spirit that resembled "The Duke."

Paranormal investigations are not allowed on the grounds of the Alamo and no electronic equipment, such as EMFs or video cameras, is permitted inside the Alamo.

Portrait of Davy Crockett by John Gadsby Chapman

Visitor Information

300 Alamo Plaza
San Antonio, Texas 78299
www.thealamo.org

The Alamo is open every day except Christmas Eve and Christmas Day. Visitors may tour what's left of the barracks and chapel. Or take a virtual tour at http://www.thealamo.org/visit/grounds/virtual-tour/alamo-vtour/index.html. After hours tours are available for groups of twenty or more (www.thealamo.org). There is also a gift shop. Across the street is the IMAX Theater, which offers a good film, The Price of Freedom. Additionally, you may want to visit The San Antonio Missions National Park, which includes four other Spanish missions.
https://www.nps.gov/saan/index.htm

San Antonio is three hours from Houston, TX (197 miles); 8.5 hours from Little Rock, AR (593 miles); and 13 hours from Tallahassee, FL (905 miles).

White House

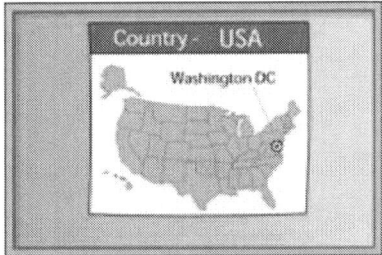

Washington, DC (District of Columbia) is the capitol of the United States and The White House is the home of the President of the United States.

A Ghost Hunter's Guide to the Most Haunted Historic Sites in America

White House

FUN FACTS:

There have been many séances held in the White House as some occupants have tried to connect with its resident ghosts.

The White House has been home to every President since John Adams in 1800.

The most haunted area is the Lincoln bedroom, but there are many other haunted areas throughout the White House. The Executive Mansion includes 132 rooms, 35 bathrooms, and six levels in the residence. There are three elevators, 8 staircases, 28 fireplaces, and 412 doors.

The History

It was built from 1792 – 1800. It was set on fire by the British Army during the War of 1812. While most of the interior was destroyed, the exterior was not too badly damaged and was soon repaired.

When Teddy Roosevelt was president, he had all the offices moved to a new addition he authorized called the West Wing. The West Wing was enlarged during William Taft's presidency. He also added the Oval Office and the East Wing. Thomas Jefferson added grandiose colonnades, which connected the two wings.

Each president added his personal touches, ranging from subtle to drastic changes. Today, the White House is a complex that includes the Blair House (guest house), East Wing, Eisenhower Executive Office Building, West Wing, and main house. The main house is six stories: ground, state, second, third, and a two-story basement.

The White House is a National Heritage Site owned by the National Park Service. Here are ten fun facts about the White House (provided by the White House Historical Association):

1. George Washington is the only president never to have slept in the White House.

2. The total cost of the original structure was $232,372.

3. The White House was the largest house in the United States until after the Civil War.

4. Today, the home's square footage is about 55,000. It features six levels, eight staircases, three elevators, 28 fireplaces and 132 rooms, including 35 bathrooms.

5. The White House grounds and garden crew consist of 13 full-time staff members, and there are five full-time chefs.

6. The nation's Executive Mansion officially became known as the White House during the administration of Theodore Roosevelt, who directed that all government correspondence use the title.

7. Benjamin Harrison brought the first Christmas tree inside in 1889.

8. The property features a tennis court, a bowling alley, a movie theater, a beauty salon, a physician's office, a florist's shop, a swimming pool and a golf putting green. Dwight Eisenhower had the first putting green installed. Richard Nixon and his wife, Pat, were avid bowlers. A jogging track was added around the driveway of the South grounds during Bill Clinton's first term.

9. The White House was designated a National Historic Landmark in 1960.

10. Each president sits for a portrait that is added to the presidential collection housed in the White House.

The Hauntings

There are many reportedly haunted areas of the White House, but it is hard to prove or disprove these reports given that ghost investigations are not permitted. However, we do have some evidence and a "top ten" list of the most haunted areas of the White House.

Yellow Oval Room

Haunt Spot #10: Yellow Oval Room. During Lincoln's administration, this room was his personal library and one of his favorite rooms in the White House. Numerous White House employees have reportedly seen Lincoln gazing out the windows of this room. First Lady Grace Coolidge also claimed to have seen him here. First Lady Mary Todd Lincoln also reported seeing the ghosts of both Presidents Thomas Jefferson and John Tyler here.

Haunt Spot #9: The Attic. President William Henry Harrison only held office for one month before dying of pneumonia. A spirit lingers in the attic, seemingly searching for something. More than a few presidents have reported hearing noises coming from the attic over the Oval Office to their Secret Service detail. No one is ever found, but some believe the noises are attributed to the ghost of Harrison, who may feel he didn't do his duty while alive, so his spirit is serving the rest of his term—and then some!

Haunt Spot #8: Rose Garden. The Rose Garden was conceived by First Lady Dolley Madison. When First Lady Ellen Wilson requested the garden be dug out during her tenure one hundred years later, the ghost of Dolley Madison appeared in the garden. And every time workers tried to fulfill Wilson's request, her spirit appeared or made its presence known. The First Lady's plan to destroy the garden was abandoned and there were no more sightings of Dolley Madison in the Rose Garden.

Haunt Spot #7: The Basement. Isn't it always haunted? But this basement is haunted by a phantom cat. It rarely appears but when it does it is to signal a national disaster. It has appeared before the great stock market crash and Great Depression, before John F. Kennedy's assassination, and other momentous occasions.

Haunt Spot #6: Second Floor Hall. This hall is part of the residence of the first family. Lincoln has been seen in these hallways by Lady Eleanor Roosevelt, President Truman, and President Taft claims to have seen First Lady Abigail Adams disappearing through a door.

Haunt Spot #5: Second Floor Bedroom. President Johnson's daughter, Lynda, claimed she saw the ghost of Abraham Lincoln's son. Willie died in the same bedroom that Lynda was using. Ghostly screams have been heard on occasion, which some believe belong to President Grove Cleveland's wife, who gave birth in this room.

Haunt Spot #4: North Portico. A British soldier has been seen here. He is carrying a torch, presumably the spirit of a soldier who was sent here during the War of 1812 to burn the White House. The ghost of Anne Surratt is also seen here. She was the daughter of Mary Surratt, who was hanged for her part in Lincoln's assassination. The ghost of Anne Surratt is sometimes heard pounding on the door, begging for her mother's life to be spared and sitting on the front steps on the anniversary of her mother's execution.

Haunt Spot #3: East Room. It is haunted by the ghost of Abigail Adams, who used it as her laundry room. An apparition is seen carrying a basket that resembles a vintage laundry basket. In 2002, a group of tourists witnessed this sight. The smell of laundry soap is also detected sometimes even though it has been a long time since laundry was done in this room—or since a first lady was tasked with laundry duty!

Haunt Spot #2: Rose Room. Sightings of President Andrew Johnson are seen in this room. He is heard cussing or laughing. There is an unexplainable cold spot in the room. Lincoln has been glimpsed in this room on occasion. Queen Wilhelmina of the Netherlands heard a knock at the door while she was sleeping in this room. When she answered it, she saw Abraham Lincoln disappearing down the hallway.

Lincoln's Bedroom

Haunt Spot #1: The most haunted area in the White House is Lincoln's Bedroom. Winston Churchill refused to sleep in the bedroom again after seeing the ghost of Abraham Lincoln beside the fireplace. According to the story, Churchill had just gotten out of the bath, so he was completely naked when he saw the ghost. Beyond those already listed as seeing Lincoln in other places, he has been spotted by Teddy Roosevelt, Herbert Hoover, and Dwight Eisenhower; First Ladies Jacquie Kennedy and Ladybird Johnson; and presidential children Susan Ford and Maureen Reagan (and her husband). Other guests have reported that lights in the bedroom turn on and off by themselves, and there are inexplicable cold spots in the room.

President Kennedy's Press Secretary James Haggerty swore he saw President Lincoln in the White House. President Bill Clinton's Press Secretary Mike McCurry must have had a ghostly encounter because he has publicly announced his belief that there are ghosts in the White House. Most modern day presidents won't admit they've witnessed anything paranormal. Perhaps they are worried about public perception. However, Hillary Clinton has stated that she has felt the spirits of all the people who have lived there and that the White House can be creepy at times.

White House séances were fairly common when Abraham Lincoln was president. Ulysses S. Grant allegedly took part in a séance and communicated with Willie Lincoln. Other unconfirmed séances include Nancy Reagan and Hillary Clinton.

There are many more ghostly encounters reported by White House staff over the years. There are also other ghosts who supposedly haunt the most famous house in America. One such ghost is David Burns. He was forced to give up his land so that the White House could be built. Some believe he never left his property. One thing is for sure. There is no disputing the fact that the White House is one of the most haunted historic sites in America.

Visitor Information

Requests for the White House tour must be submitted through your Member of Congress (https://www.whitehouse.gov/participate/tours-and-events). These self-guided tours are available in the morning Tuesday through Saturday. Tour hours are extended whenever possible as the White House schedule permits. Tours are scheduled on a first come, first served basis. You can submit a request up to six months in advance of your visit. The earlier, the better as only a limited number of spaces are available.

The White House will notify your Congressional Representative of your tour request status approximately two weeks before the tour date. Spring and summer tours fill up quickly, so make your request early. Want to see the holiday decorations? You can begin to submit your Christmas tour request in June. All tours are free of charge.

A list of the requirements and restrictions is provided on the website. A free, online **White House Tour** is also available on their website.

The **White House Garden Tour** is offered twice a year over weekends in the spring and fall.

At this time, the only way to experience a **West Wing Tour** is by invitation from the White House or through a personal connection to a White House staffer willing to lead you on an after-hours tour. But you can download an official West Wing Tour Booklet at https://whitehouse.gov1.info/visit/tour.html#westwing.

1600 Pennsylvania Ave NW, Washington, DC 20500

https://whitehouse.gov1.info/visit/tour.html

Washington, DC is one hour and forty-five minutes from Richmond, VA (110 miles); 9 hours from Indianapolis, IN (577 miles); and 4 hours from Raleigh, NC (283 miles).

A Ghost Hunter's Guide to the Most Haunted Historic Sites in America

Battleship North Carolina

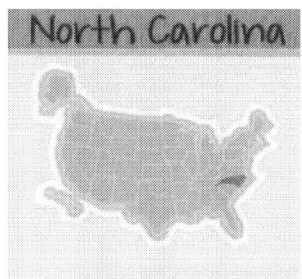

Battleship North Carolina

FUN FACTS:

The ship was involved in every major naval offensive during WWII.

Five men died when the ship was torpedoed on September 15, 1942. The spirits of these men may still be aboard.

The ship was like a floating city. A library, brig (jail), mess hall, galley, church, barber shop, sick bay, bakery, post office, and butcher shop are on board.

The History

Battleship NC being towed into Wilmington harbor in 1961

The roughly 40,000-ton battleship was first used during World War II. When she was commissioned on April 9, 1941, she was considered to be the world's greatest sea weapon. The *Battleship NC* was the first battleship built in the U.S. in sixteen years. It was the first of ten great ships that were commissioned: *Washington, South Dakota, Indiana, Massachusetts, Alabama, Iowa, New Jersey, Missouri, and Wisconsin.*

The battleship was equipped with a lot of firepower, including nine 16-inch/45 caliber guns; twenty 5-inch/38 caliber guns; sixty 40mm/56 caliber guns; and forty-eight 20mm/70 caliber guns. During WWII, the nine-deck ship participated in every major naval offensive in the Pacific and earned fifteen battle stars, as well as eight medals and citations. During the war, close to 2,200 enlisted men and 144 commissioned officers served aboard the vessel. Ten men died during the war (and 67 men were injured).

After it had been decommissioned on June 27, 1947, the ship sat in New Jersey for fourteen years as part of an Inactive Reserve Fleet. Plans to scrap the ship brought cries of protest from North Carolina citizens, who subsequently launched the SOS (Save Our Ship) Campaign. Devoted North Carolinians, including schoolchildren who donated part of their lunch money, raised $330,000. Interestingly, the ship cost $76,885,750 to build. The ship arrived "home" to Wilmington's harbor in October 1961. The ship, nicknamed "Showboat," was declared a

National Historic Landmark in 1986 and is considered a museum ship, which is on the National Register of Historic Places.

The Hauntings

At least some of the men who died while serving on the battleship are believed to be aboard still—as ghosts! The ship's night watchman, visitors who had strange experiences during their tours, and several highly respectable ghost hunting organizations, including *Haunted North Carolina* and SyFy's *Ghost Hunters* (T.A.P.S.) believe the vessel is haunted.

It was a well-kept secret for many years, probably because only one man has been onboard most nights. The night watchman, Danny Bradshaw, is one of the few people to have access to the ship during the night. If there is any truth to what he says, the ship is a scary place to be after hours. The first time he saw a ghost, Bradshaw was on his way to the galley during his nightly rounds. Since the lights are turned off at night for economy, he used a flashlight to find his way. The beam revealed a shocking sight in the mess hall. He saw sailors standing in line to be served their evening meal! The faces were shadowy, but there was no doubt the men were wearing uniforms. As he tried to register what he was witnessing, he suddenly felt cold, and a hand touched his shoulder. When he whirled around to see what was going on, he saw nothing. But he did hear departing footsteps.

The frightened security guard used the flashlight to search the room. Bradshaw nearly fainted with fear at what the beam of light revealed. A young blond sailor stood staring at him from an open hatch. He didn't pause. He turned and hurried to the ladder. Bradshaw began climbing to the next deck, determined to get out of there as quickly as possible. He stopped when he heard banging coming from the overhead deck where he was headed. He nearly forgot to breathe as he heard footsteps above him. The night watchman reversed direction and scurried back down the ladder. He soon found another ladder and ascended it without incident.

Bradshaw believes there are at least two ghosts aboard the ship. One just slams doors, moves objects, and turns lights on and off. The other ghost is not so harmless. The room gets very cold when the evil presence appears. The ghost sometimes yells at Bradshaw and chases him.

The paranormal reports from Bradshaw, visitors, and other employees have drawn the attention of ghost investigators who brought their knowledge and equipment to find out if there was any truth to the stories.

The most haunted areas of the ship are the port bow, engine room, sick bay, shower room, and mess hall. The night watchman reports that doors and hatches open and close by themselves, and sometimes lights and televisions turn on and off on their own. Footsteps and voices can be heard, but no one is there. Cold spots have been felt, and objects have inexplicably been moved.

When SyFy's *Ghost Hunters* and TAPS conducted their two-night investigation, their thermal cameras picked up activity. An EVP was captured in the brig area. EMF readings also registered activity. The team, headed up by Jason Hawes and Grant Wilson, heard voices, footsteps, and some banging that could not be explained. Hatchways opened and closed without any logical explanation. And there was other inexplicable noises and activity.

The most incredible event witnessed during the investigation was when Hawes and Wilson saw a shadowy figure, which they pursued. They never found anyone, yet there was no exit. Anyone that went down that hallway would have had to be inside the room it led to or turn around and come back the same way—unless what they saw wasn't human?

Another team member witnessed another sighting. Hawthorne swore he saw a shadowy figure peeking out from behind a locker. He tried to take a photo but it whatever he saw was gone by the time he got his camera in position.

There was a great deal of activity the night of their investigation. Besides all the abnormal readings, noises, and disappearing figure they saw, a portal door slammed shut behind a couple of the team members. But no one in the group was responsible. Another inexplicable event was camera movement. An infrared camera was mounted on the aft of the ship. The stationary camera often moved on its own!

Other groups have investigated this ship, including *Haunted North Carolina* and *RDU Ghost Trackers*. *Haunted NC* heard so much knocking during their investigation that they asked the spirit(s) if they would give one knock for "yes" and two knocks for "no" to their questions. During their first round of questions, they heard an unmistakable and unexplainable knock. It seemed to come from the area to the left of the questioner's head.

The results of all these investigations indicate paranormal activity. The evidence includes EVPs, EMFs, and credible eyewitness reports, which includes supernatural sounds and sightings.

Visitor Information

The ship is moored at Wilmington's harbor, on Eagles Island, which is linked to the mainland by a causeway. The battleship sits on the New Hanover-Brunswick County line, located at the junction of Highways 17, 74, 76 and 421. There are two ways to get there, by car or by hiring a water taxi that departs from the historic district. Boat departs from the foot of Market Street. There's a gift shop, snack bar, museum, and picnic area at the end of the large parking lot. The ship is open to the public, and much of the ship can be toured. Special events are held on board year round. Additionally, the vessel can be rented for special occasions or private ghost investigations.

Battleship North Carolina
#1 Battleship Road
Wilmington, NC 28401
www.battleshipnc.com

Wilmington is 2 hours from Raleigh, NC (132 miles); 4 hours and forty-five minutes from Newport News, VA (290 miles); and 6 hours from Atlanta, GA (416 miles).

Terrance Zepke

Alcatraz

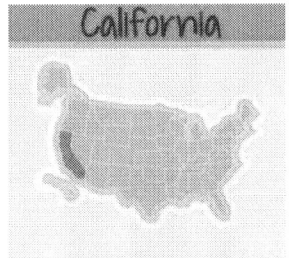

A Ghost Hunter's Guide to the Most Haunted Historic Sites in America

Alcatraz

FUN FACTS

It has been nicknamed "The Rock" and made famous by Hollywood movies, such as these classics: The Birdman of Alcatraz (1962); Escape from Alcatraz (1979); Seven Miles from Alcatraz (1942); and The Rock (1996). Fox Television aired a mysterious weekly drama called "Alcatraz" in 2012.

The prison housed more than 1,000 criminals. There were fourteen escape attempts with only one man making it to shore. He was soon captured near the Golden Gate Bridge. Some bodies were never found but presumed drowned in the rough, icy waters. It is ironic that it was known as the worst prison but had the best food!

Roughly 1.3 million people visit Alcatraz annually. Besides being a historic site, it is home to many nesting birds, marine life, and rare plants and flowers.

The History

The site became a federal prison in 1934. For twenty-nine years, it was an impregnable fortress that housed the worst criminals in America. During its time as a military fortress, there were more than 100 cannons at Alcatraz.

Because it is an island surrounded by fierce wind, treacherous currents, and icy water, prisoners had little hope of escape. These conditions made the island the perfect place to put hardcore criminals who were a danger to society and considered "unredeemable."

Its origin dates back to the late 1700s when Spanish explorers discovered the island, naming it "La Isla de los Alcatraces" (Island of Pelicans). Alcatraz was first used by the U.S. government in the mid-1800s as a military fortress. During this time, relations between America and Mexico were continuous. On June 1, 1854, the first lighthouse on the island was lit. Its light could be seen up to eighteen miles away. This was also the first lighthouse on the West Coast.

By 1860, Alcatraz had become more than a fortress. It also served as a military prison. During the Civil War, roughly fifty Confederate sympathizers and deserters were imprisoned here. The conditions were deplorable. The men had to sleep in cramped quarters—head to toe—on the floor. The prison had no heat, no insulation, no running water, no bathrooms, and the food was rationed. Disease, such as scurvy and lice, was rampant.

During the Civil War, it became the largest fort west of the Mississippi River. After the Civil War, more cells and buildings were added. In the latter part of the 1800s, many Indian chiefs and tribal leaders were brought to Alcatraz for refusing to give up their land. They were forced to share quarters with the dregs of society: rapists, thieves, and criminals who had been captured after escaping from other facilities.

By 1898, the population had swelled to close to 500, thanks to the Spanish-American War. In the 1900s, it also became a military detention center. Soldiers who were disciplined for military infractions were brought to Alcatraz. Their punishment included rations, hard labor, and solitary confinement. Interestingly, the prison also became a recovery center for soldiers who had contracted tropical diseases while stationed in places like Cuba and the Philippines. Hard to think of Alcatraz as a convalescence facility!

Because it was used for so many purposes, Alcatraz soon became overcrowded. Because of harsh weather conditions and its age, Alcatraz was also desperately in need of renovations. Construction began in earnest in 1904 to repair and add onto the facility. Despite the Great Earthquake of 1906, the mammoth project was completed in 1909. The prison now had a new kitchen, dining hall, library, bath house, and lighthouse.

Once again, Alcatraz accommodated prisoners-of-war during World War I. Eventually, the minimum security prison became antiquated and was in danger of being closed down for good. But the 1920s and 1930s brought a resurgence of crime. FBI Chief J. Edgar Hoover tried to stop widespread crime by declaring Alcatraz a maximum security prison for hardened criminals.

As part of this plan, the prison became part of the Federal Bureau of Prisons in 1933. Metal detectors, barbed wire, electric locks, and gun towers were added. The former keeper's house became the warden's residence. More guards were hired so that the ratio was 3:1 guards to prisoners and apartments built on the island to house their families. For twenty-nine years, the facility housed notorious gang leaders and other tough criminals. This is the era that made Alcatraz legendary.

But by the early 1960s, the facility was once again in need of major renovations. The salt and cold and the wind caused significant deterioration to everything on the island. On March 23, 1963, the prison was closed permanently. It sat vacant until 1969 before a group of Native American Indians tried to lay claim to it. In 1970, a fire destroyed the old keeper's house and damaged many buildings, including the lighthouse. It was never proven, but the government believed the fire was set by Indian activists. In 1973, the former fortress and prison was opened to the public.

Pictured here was the recreation area of Alcatraz. Image courtesy of NPS.

ALCATRAZ TIMELINE:

The late 1700s: Spanish explorer discovered the island.

1854: A fort and lighthouse were built by U.S. Army. It was originally located near the dock. The lighthouse was the first one built on the West Coast. During the Civil War, this fort was the largest Union fort west of the Mississippi River, housing mainly war prisoners.

1907: Alcatraz was officially designated a military prison.

1909: Construction completed on new cellhouse and buildings on the island. Old prison and lighthouse demolished.

1933 Alcatraz was transferred to Federal Bureau of Prisons.

1933-1963 Alcatraz was a federal prison.

1963: The prison closed permanently.

1969: It was occupied by Native American Indians who wanted to turn it into an Indian Cultural Center. They held the island for nineteen months before federal marshals forcibly removed them. An Indian girl died from a fall while staying with her stepfather during the occupation.

1970: Fire damaged Alcatraz.

1972: Alcatraz became part of the NPS Golden Gate Recreation Area.

1973: Alcatraz opened to the public.

2015: A $3 million restoration was completed on the guardhouse, library and schoolhouse structures. Now visitors can see the building's original entrance sign reading "Alcatraces 1857."

According to one park ranger, the Birdman was the worst prisoner at Alcatraz. He insisted on shaving his entire body and guards were forced to supervise this ritual. They said he stared at them the entire time that he showered and shaved. Too creepy!

The Hauntings

Places where great suffering and sadness occurs, such as hospitals, asylums, and prisons, are often haunted by forlorn spirits. It should come as no surprise that Alcatraz is haunted. Inside the cell block, strange sounds are often heard by the night watchmen. There is a utility corridor where three men were shot while trying to escape that is one of the most haunted places at Alcatraz. National Park Service personnel and night watchmen have witnessed ghostly sightings, the smell of smoke, and all kinds of noises: phantom gunshots, banging, banjo music (while imprisoned at Alcatraz, Al Capone played banjo in a prison band), clanging, screaming, footsteps, moaning, disembodied voices, and sobbing.

Employees quickly for the source of the gunshots or smoke or screams, but never find anything. These strange incidents happen so often, especially late in the day or at night, that employees seldom report them anymore. There are several haunted areas, including the Warden's House, the hospital, the laundry room, the utility corridor, and the cell blocks. But Cell 14D is reportedly one of the most haunted places. Visitors have complained about how much colder it is than anywhere else in the building—even in the middle of summer!

Inmates who were put into "The Hole" (solitary confinement) complained of a ghostly presence, but it may have just been their minds playing tricks on them. Or there may have been a sinister spirit sharing their quarters. One man was found dead in the cell the next morning after screaming half the night about a "creature with glowing eyes." He appeared to have been strangled. The autopsy revealed that this was not self-inflicted. If the inmate confined to solitary confinement was found strangled and it was not done by his own hands then how did it happen? The incident remains unsolved. Other prisoners have reported the presence of a man dressed in clothing from the late 1800s walking the hallway next to these cells.

Cell 14D is one of six cells dubbed as "The Hole" on the lower level D block. This was punishment for prisoners who had broken the rules. Prisoners were kept here in complete isolation for up to nineteen days. The only amenities were a toilet, low watt lightbulb, sink, and mattress, which was provided only at night. These 'holes' were also known as strip cells because a prisoner was stripped of his clothing and all reading material for the duration of his time served. These were dark, damp solitude cells. One of the six cells was considered the worst one because it had no sink or toilet—just a hole in the floor. No wonder this is one of the most haunted areas of the prison! Reportedly, some guards refused to go into this area alone.

Sightings of prisoner and soldier spirits have been seen by visitors, employees, and family members of employees. Once, the warden himself had a ghostly encounter. While walking through the prison, he heard sobbing from inside the dungeon walls and suddenly felt abnormally cold. Park rangers have heard cell doors slamming shut and opening at night for no logical reason. These doors operate by key lock and park rangers have the only keys. So how could these locked doors suddenly open on their own? Over the years, many tourists have claimed to have found ghostly images on the photos they took while at Alcatraz. Some can be found on YouTube if you search for 'ghosts' and 'Alcatraz.'

Back in the early 1980's, a psychic named Jeanne Borgen and a well-known broadcaster, Ted Wygant, spent the night at Alcatraz. Wygant's goal was to debunk the existence of ghosts. A camera crew and park rangers accompanied the pair throughout the night. In the wee hours of the morning, Borden and Wygant were investigating the utility corridor when a strange feeling overcame both of them. They suddenly felt extremely agitated and angry. Wygant began screaming profanities and Borgen grew violent. The pair did not calm down until they were led out of the area. The utility corridor is one of the most haunted places in Alcatraz, presumably became this is where the most bloodshed occurred. Two guards and three inmates were killed here during an escape attempt. Wygant and Borden became "possessed" with a feeling of evil soon after calling out the names of one of the inmates who was killed during this escape attempt. When Travel Channel's *Ghost Adventures* investigated, they also endured a "hateful energy." You can see what they caught on camera at http://www.travelchannel.com/shows/ghost-adventures/episodes/alcatraz.

Capital Area Paranormal Society conducted an investigation in 2014. They recorded several interesting EVPs. You can hear those recordings at http://www.capsinvestigations.com/alcatraz-island. To see the results of the American Paranormal Research Association's 2010 investigation, visit https://www.youtube.com/watch?v=EhRVyEKQd78.

Alcatraz (also known as Hellcatraz) was considered to be one of the most secure prisons in the world. In fact, no successful escape has ever been confirmed. There have been fourteen attempts and all involved were apprehended, drowned, or shot and killed except three who remain unaccounted for. These men are believed to have drowned but their bodies were never recovered. While there were no known successful escapes, murder did occur at Alcatraz. An inmate murdered another inmate, a mob hitman named Abie "Butcher" Maldowitz. Many believe his spirit still haunts Alcatraz. Al Capone was so fearful of being executed that he got special permission to practice his banjo in the shower room while the other men enjoyed recreational time in the yard. Some refute that Capone was permitted a banjo, but there is nothing in the official records to confirm or dispute this claim.

Many psychics have visited Alcatraz and all have reported psychic experiences while on the island. One psychic, Nancy Osborn, went so far as to say that she had never felt so much psychic energy in one place until her visit to Alcatraz. Some of these psychics felt cold hands on their necks and had visions of a tall, bald man with beady eyes. That matches the description of Abie "Butcher" Maldowitz. Some of the men who died while trying to escape, such as Joseph Cretzer and Bernard Coy, are believed to haunt Alcatraz.

Most Famous Prisoners:

Al Capone, Doc Barker of the Ma Barker Gang, George "Machine Gun" Kelly, Robert "Birdman of Alcatraz" Stroud, Floyd Hamilton of Bonnie and Clyde Gang, and James "Tex" Lucas (who tried to kill Al Capone and made a violent escape attempt from Alcatraz that included beating a guard to death).

Visitor Information:

Alcatraz Island, Golden Gate National Recreation Area
Fort Mason, B201
San Francisco, CA 94123

Tours depart from Alcatraz Landing Pier 33. However, the only parking is for the handicapped. However, there is some street parking and commercial parking lots in the area where visitors may pay to park.

The official NPS website is www.nps.gov/alca/index.htm.

Other helpful NPS sites include www.nps.gov/goga and www.nps.gov/alcatraz

For transportation to the island, you can use the NPS ferry or opt for a cruise tour, such as www.alcatrazcruises.com, which includes an audio tour that is available in many languages. Most folks don't realize that there are lovely gardens on the island. If interested in this option, contact www.alcatrazgardens.org. Whatever tour method you choose, plan to spend a minimum of 2-3 hours including the ride to the island.

The island is steep and hilly, so wear good walking shoes and be prepared to walk roughly a quarter of a mile from the dock to the prison, which is at the top of the island. For those unable to make this steep ascent, there is SEAT (Sustainable Easy Access Transport). The electric shuttle transports passengers from the dock to the prison. Even hardy souls may want to utilize it when the cold wind is blowing, but be aware that it has limited hours of operation and those with limited mobility are given priority. Come prepared for any weather as it can be nice or windy or cold or foggy. While the weather is unpredictable on Alcatraz, be advised that the best time is April-June and September-October. During the summer, there is often heavy fog. Visitors should wear sunscreen and bring a raincoat/jacket and a hat.

San Francisco is 25.5 hours from Dallas, TX (1,739 miles); 5 hours and forty-five minutes from Los Angeles, CA (382 miles); and 8 hours and forty-five minutes from Las Vegas, NV (572 miles).

FYI: Overnight visits are permitted, but they are expensive and awarded by lottery only. Groups must fill out a National Park Service Overnight Application. These applications are received November 1-30. Overnight visits are scheduled for March – December.

Terrance Zepke

Statue of Liberty & Ellis Island

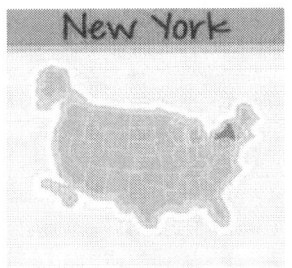

A Ghost Hunter's Guide to the Most Haunted Historic Sites in America

Statue of Liberty and Ellis Island

Statue of Liberty in background and part of Ellis Island Immigration Museum in foreground

FUN FACTS:

More than two million people explore Ellis Island and its museum every year.

Many died here within an arm's grasp of freedom. Perhaps that's why these spirits are unable to leave this place?

Captain Kidd reportedly still guards his pirate treasure.

The History

While most of us think of Ellis Island as being synonymous with the Statue of Liberty that is not correct. The Statue of Liberty is on Liberty Island, not Ellis Island. But both are symbols of freedom.

It is incredible to think that nearly thirteen million people were processed through Ellis Island from 1824 – 1924. But for every immigrant who achieved his dream, there were many who did not. Many arrived ill from the arduous journey across the ocean. Many were in questionable mental and physical condition upon arrival and had to be evaluated and treated. These men, women, and children had to be detained until their status could be determined.

Some were treated and soon released. Some required a lengthy recuperation. Some were incurable. Records reveal that 3,500 people died on Ellis Island. One reference claims that one in five immigrants was detained at Ellis Island Immigrant Hospital. And there wasn't always a happy ending. Some were sent back home while others died on route, or soon after arrival.

Sadly, the final days of some of these immigrants were spent in isolation. They were quarantined to prevent the spread of contagious diseases. Families often had to keep going without a loved one and this included children. The journey was hardest on the very young and the old. Those who were known to be contagious or suspected of being contagious were transferred by a medical boat to the island hospital. Imagine how horrible it would have been—stuck in a dark, crowded steerage compartment for weeks on end only to end up being whisked away to a hospital ward before you even had a chance to see the Statue of Liberty.

Speaking of which, the Status of Liberty commemorates the signing of the Declaration of Independence. It was given to America by France as a symbol of freedom and friendship, following the American Revolution. The statue is made of copper, and the torch is coated in gold leaf. Including the pedestal and foundation, the statue is 305 feet tall. It is part of the State of Liberty National Monument, which includes Ellis Island. Rumors abound that like Ellis Island; it too is haunted.

The Hauntings

During the daytime, the Statue of Liberty is as quiet as a graveyard, but when darkness arrives, the sounds begin. The statue is comprised of giant copper bronze plates riveted together. These plates contract when they get wet. This contraction creates an indescribable sound, a combination of groaning and rattling. On a night when the dampness is especially bad, the groaning and rattling can be dreadful. Despite the logical explanation, night watchmen often get so spooked that they quit rather than endure another night of standing in the dark listening to these eerie noises. The watchmen grow convinced the explanation is more supernatural than rational. Many boaters who have passed near the island on a particularly damp (and noisy) night, tend to agree.

But some speculate the Statue of Liberty is haunted by Captain William Kidd. Before this pirate (who swore to his dying breath that he was privateer) was hanged for piracy in 1701, he reportedly buried a substantial treasure he brought back from his legendary three-year treasure hunt. According to legend, he had planned to use it to bribe officials into dropping piracy charges. It was a good plan given that these were greedy men. But Captain Kidd miscalculated how much things had changed during his three-year absence. A zero tolerance policy on piracy had happened while he was gone.

Before his arrest, Kidd allegedly hid gold and jewels and other valuables all along the eastern seaboard. Many believe it was buried on Liberty Island (near Kidd's house on Pearl Street) and protected by Captain Kidd himself! According to legend, some soldiers stationed at Fort Wood, who had heard this story, went in search of the treasure. They followed directions given to them by a psychic. Their efforts paid off. They dug up a chest. It was a big, old wooden chest. Could this be Kidd's treasure? Before they could find out, a spirit appeared in pirate garb brandishing a shiny cutlass. He was so real looking, the men got spooked and ran away. The next day, they returned to claim the chest. It was gone! In its place was a skull. They left and never returned. I do not believe this ghost story, but you can choose to believe it if you like.

I believe Ellis Island is haunted. Over the years, lots of strange things have happened on the island, especially in the Ellis Island Immigration Museum. Park rangers and visitors have heard the sound of furniture being moved, crying, and doors opening and closing. But no one is ever found when someone goes to check out the noises. Former Chief Ranger, Dean Garrett, once heard some children talking in the Great Hall. Thinking maybe it was kids on a field trip, he went into the room to greet the children. The room was empty! Some visitors have complained of a strange sensation overcoming them while in the museum. Could it be empathy for the immigrants or could the explanation be more supernatural?

But almost no one has access to what is the most haunted place on the island—the hospital. The once beautiful, hospital complex is now in ruins. The impressive copper, marble, and terra cotta accents are barely recognizable anymore. It is not safe for staff or visitors to walk these decaying hallways. But it is likely that the ghosts of those who suffered so before succumbing to death still linger, especially in the old operating room, nursery, psychiatric ward and morgue.

Ellis Island

Visitor Information

The tour is self-guided and can take 3-5 hours depending on your pace and if you visit the museum and the entire statue or just the grounds, pedestal, or a crown tour. Note that crown tours sell out so book well in advance, if interested. Visitors will have to undergo a security screening before they are permitted to board the ferry. The statue and museum are under the supervision of the National Park Service. They are national monuments.

Here are some tips for an optimum experience:

*Visitors can depart from Battery Park (NY) and Liberty State Park (NJ).

*Arrive at least thirty minutes before your scheduled time. NOTE THAT DURING PEAK TIMES, WAIT TIMES TO BOARD THE FERRY CAN BE AN HOUR OR LONGER. You will be screened by security before you are permitted to board the boat.

*Flip flops, sandals and open-toe shoes are not allowed on the Hard Hat tour. Keep in mind that you will be inside and outside, so dress accordingly.

*The boats are handicapped accessible. There are restrooms and concessions aboard the boat.

*The statue is open daily year round, except Christmas Day. More than three million people visit the statue every year.

https://www.statuecruises.com

Statue of Liberty

Liberty Island, NY 10004

https://www.nps.gov/stli/planyourvisit/hours.htm

Webcam of statue:
http://earthcam.com/cams/newyork/statueofliberty//?cam=liberty_str

Free mobile tour app: https://www.nps.gov/stli/planyourvisit/free-mobile-app.htm

Ellis Island Immigration Museum has three floors of exhibits. There are free, ranger-guided tours that last approximately thirty minutes.

Hard Hat Tours are guided ninety-minute tours will take you to select areas of the Ellis Island Hospital Complex. There is a fee, and you should make reservations in advance. No one under the age of thirteen is permitted on these tours. https://www.statuecruises.com/statue-liberty-and-ellis-island-tickets#/

Ellis Island, NY 10004

https://www.nps.gov/elis/index.htm

New York City is 3 hours from Harrisburg, PA (173 miles); 12 hours from Charleston, SC (763 miles); and 75 minutes from Trenton, NJ (67 miles).

Terrance Zepke

Mammoth Cave

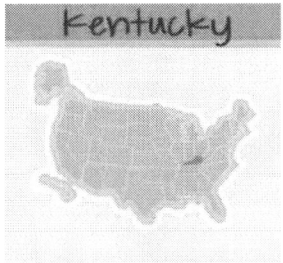

A Ghost Hunter's Guide to the Most Haunted Historic Sites in America

Mammoth Cave

FUN FACTS:

This is the largest cave in the world and twice as large as the second biggest cave in the world, which is in Mexico.

The cave once housed a TB hospital.

Mammoth Cave is the most haunted cave in America.

The History

Mammoth Cave includes 392 miles of caves that date back roughly fifteen million years. Interestingly, the cave has served for many purposes, such as being mined for nitrates, which are used for making gunpowder. It has also been used as a hospital, Indian burial ground, for saltpeter production, and as a tourist attraction. In fact, it is one of North America's oldest tourist attractions.

During the late 1800s, there was a billiard hall and dining area in the cave. It housed a mushroom farm for a few years. There was even a Mammoth Cave Hotel at one time. It consisted of a dining room, ballroom, and a dozen guest rooms. The log building burned down in 1916. There were plans to erect a hotel inside the cave, but that never happened. Locals once used the cave as cold storage for their milk and produce. Moonshiners hid their stills in the cave. It was a favorite play area for area children.

Mammoth Cave became a national park in 1926. As such, all the underground caves became protected. This meant that private property owners who wouldn't sell their land (which included part of this cave system), had it seized by the government in the name of eminent domain law.

One of the former TB huts in Mammoth Cave

 **The Hauntings**

Native Americans used this cave system to bury their dead. Many of these "mummies" have been discovered in the last several decades. They are well-preserved due to the climate and conditions of the cave. The deceased were still "posed" in their burial positions. It is believed by many that the spirits of these Native Americans still haunt Mammoth Cave.

The cave system was used as a TB hospital in the 1800s. The remains of eleven consumptive (a synonym for tuberculosis) cabins can still be seen today. Sadly, this was a failed experiment since all fifteen TB patients died while here, including the founder of the cave clinic, Dr. John Croghan. It is believed these tortured spirits linger here where they died so tragically. What else could explain the phantom coughing that is often heard in this part of the cave? Be sure to listen closely when you get near Corpse Rock, and you may just hear or see something yourself.

As word spread about this spectacular cave system, the cave became a huge tourist destination. Visitors came from all over the U.S. and from as far as England and Russia. Many celebrities have explored this cave, such as Ralph Waldo Emerson and Russia's Prince Alexis. Slaves were used as tour guides before the Civil War. Park rangers have reported seeing apparitions resembling slave guides.

Stephan Bishop was a cave explorer and slave guide. He loved the cave so much that he may still be here. His spirit is sometimes seen by participants of the evening lantern tour. He was once quoted as saying that Mammoth Cave is "A grand, gloomy and peculiar place." He is buried in Old Guide Cemetery, which is near the cave entrance.

One tragic story involves a young woman named Melissa. She confessed her sad story on her deathbed. She was in love with a young man, Beverleigh, from Boston. He was her tutor. Unfortunately, he was not in love with her. When Beverleigh began dating another girl, Melissa felt rejected and furious. Hell hath no fury like a woman scorned! She lured Beverleigh to the cave in 1843 on some pretense of a tour. When she got deep into the cave (near Purgatory Point), she slipped away. Poor Beverleigh was left to find his way out on his own. When Melissa learned that Beverleigh hadn't been seen since she'd left him in the cave, she went back for him. She searched all day but to no avail. She kept searching the cave for days but never found any sign of Beverleigh. In fact, he was never seen again. Melissa was devastated by the outcome of her cruel prank. She kept the terrible secret until she was about to die of tuberculosis. It is said that her spirit still searches the cave for her lost love.

    There have been more than 150 documented cases of paranormal activity have been recorded here. The spookiest spots in the cave are Giant's Coffin, TB Cabins, Devil's Looking Glass, and Mummy Ledge (where LOST JOHN mummy found in 1935). Visitors have been grabbed, touched and pushed by invisible forces. Footsteps, cries, and muffled voices have been heard. These are believed to be the ghosts of the TB patients and slave guides.

    But the most famous story involving Mammoth Cave is about Floyd Collins. Collins had grown up exploring and playing in Mammoth Cave. He was a cave guide for many years. One day while either excavating or exploring the cave, a large boulder fell on his lower leg and foot. Floyd got pinned against the wall, unable to move the giant stone off his foot so that he could get out of the narrow passageway. During his struggle, he got into an odd position and got himself good and stuck. Luckily, his absence was soon discovered, but none of his friends or family was able to get him free. The media soon heard about the man that was stuck inside Mammoth Cave.

    Remarkably, no one was able to free him. For sixteen days all kinds of attempts were made, including pulling Floyd out regardless of possible injury, which included losing his leg and foot. All efforts failed. Unfortunately, the repeated efforts to free Collins resulted in a series of cave-ins, which caused the poor man to be even more hopelessly trapped. Rescue workers were afraid of getting trapped or killed if they continued, so all rescue efforts soon stopped. A final attempt was made with a rescue shaft. It worked! After a long, tedious process, the shaft reached Floyd. But he had already died of exhaustion and exposure.

Ever since that time, reports of a tired, dirty-looking apparition has been seen in different areas of the cave. This spirit is most often seen near the entrance to the cave, the site of his entrapment, and near the Flint Ridge Baptist Church Cemetery (twenty miles NE of Bowling Green) where he was buried, but obviously not laid to rest.

Perhaps he will never be able to rest in peace given his tragic death and what happened after his death. Due to the notoriety of this story, many tourists were drawn to the cave. The family supposedly dug up Floyd Collin's coffin and transferred his corpse into a glass coffin, which they displayed at the entrance to Crystal Cave, which Floyd once owned. Many tourists paid a pretty penny to see this glass-entombed corpse until it was stolen. Incredibly, it was eventually returned, but Floyd was missing his left leg. Who stole it and what happened to the leg remains a mystery.

Visitor Information

The park is open during the day seven days a week March – June. There is no fee to enter the park, but there is a fee to go into the cave. Golden

Age Passes are accepted. Cave tour reservations are not required but are recommended. Please note that the cave is not handicapped accessible, but the visitor center is handicapped accessible. Wear good walking shoes and bring a jacket as the average temperature inside the cave is 54°F. There is a restaurant and a snack bar inside the **Mammoth Cave Hotel**, which is the only public food option without the park. The hotel is across from the visitor's center, and there is a paved trail to the cave entrance.

In addition to the self-guided tour, visitors can opt for a special **Violet City Lantern Tour**. These tours are given by rangers carrying kerosene lanterns. Be warned these tours include climbing 160 steps!

Note: **Sand Cave Trail** is on Cave City Road. There is a boardwalk that leads to the site of Floyd Collins' entrapment in 1925.

Mammoth Cave National Park offers the Headquarters Campground, which is adjacent to the visitor center, pass). Houchins Ferry Campground is a primitive 12-site campground, and Maple Springs Group Campground is located six miles from the visitor center. It has seven campsites.

To get to the park from the north: Take I-65 to Exit 53 (Cave City Exit). Turn right onto KY-70. Follow 70/255 until it becomes Mammoth Cave Parkway, which dead ends into the visitor center.

To get to the park from the south: Take I-65 to Exit 48 (Park City Exit). Follow 255 until it becomes Park City Road, which merges into Mammoth Cave Parkway. The Parkway dead ends into the visitor center.

1 Mammoth Cave Parkway

Mammoth Cave, KY 42259

www.nps.gov/maca

Mammoth Cave is twenty miles northeast of Bowling Green; five hours from Memphis, TN (307 miles; and 6 hours from Springfield, IL (370 miles).

Terrance Zepke

Harper's Ferry

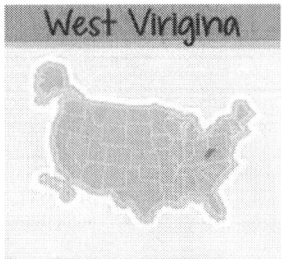

Harper's Ferry

FUN FACTS:

John Brown's Raid on Harper's Ferry was a catalyst for the Civil War.

There are at least eight ghosts in Harper's Ferry.

Harper's Ferry National Park includes the historic town of Harper's Ferry, which has a permanent population of 300.

The History

Harper's Ferry (also spelled Harpers Ferry) was first settled by Peter Stephens in 1732. George Washington chose this as the site of one of his armories. In 1859, John Brown came to Harper's Ferry. His plan was to take over the armory and create a free state for slaves. However, things didn't quite go according to plan. General Lee and his men captured John Brown and his men in less than a day. They were all sentenced to death.

But John Brown's Raid on Harper's Ferry was a major precursor to the Civil War. The Battle of Harper's Ferry was fought September 12 – 15, 1862. As General Lee's Army invaded Maryland, he sent Major General "Stonewall" Jackson to capture Harper's Ferry, which they did with little effort or casualties. But this didn't last long. In fact, the town of Harper's Ferry changed hands between the Confederates and the Union fourteen times during the Civil War.

The 4,000-acre park was established in 1944 and has been on the National Register of Historic Places since 1966. The population is less than 300 permanent residents.

Harper's Ferry Fun Facts:

*It was the starting point for Lewis & Clarke's historic expedition.

*It was the site of three Civil War battles.

*The Appalachian Trail passes through Harper's Ferry.

*It is famous for its spectacular scenery and known as the most painted town in America. It has been painted by more artists than any other place in this nation.

*It was a retreat for famous folks during the early twentieth century, including Mark Twain and several presidents.

A Ghost Hunter's Guide to the Most Haunted Historic Sites in America

John Brown Fort

The Hauntings

Ghosts have been seen at night wandering the streets of Harper's Ferry. According to witnesses, spirits are often seen entering and exiting historic properties. The one most commonly seen is a tall, lean man wearing a dark suit and bears a striking resemblance to Abolitionist John Brown. One of the spookier sights is the Phantom Army that is sometimes seen marching down Main Street. French troops were sent to Harper's Ferry in the late 1700's when war seemed imminent. However, that was a false alarm. Before they could be shipped home, most of these men died of cholera. They were buried at Camp Hill. Before they got sick, the men paraded through town every day carrying rifles and playing fifes and drums. On rare occasions, this troop has been heard by witnesses on Main Street. A few claim to see what appears to be a military troop at the end of the street, but then whatever they saw just vanishes right in front of them!

John Brown

One of the most haunted places in Harper's Ferry is the John Brown farmhouse, now known as the Kennedy Foundation. Abolitionist John Brown and his men slept in the tiny attic before the raid. The ghost of John Brown has been heard pacing this attic. The sounds of boots going up and down the stairs have also been heard. Snoring and muffled voices have been heard on occasion. Psychics sent to investigate the strange activity confirm that John Brown is still hanging out in his old hideout. His spirit has also been seen walking around the town. He even posed for a photo with some tourists, but he was not present when the photos were developed—just a space where he should have appeared!

The most haunted house is the National Park Service's guest house. Employees have encountered a well-dressed man wearing an expensive-looking vest, a top hat, and carrying a cane. He has been seen standing at the top of the stairs to the servant's quarters. Those who have seen it do not believe it is a benevolent spirit. One female park employee swears that she was pushed in the opposite direction when she was trying to leave after seeing the spirit. A female spirit has been seen on the staircase wearing a long, gray dress. She was holding the hand of a small child. Within seconds the spirits simply disappeared.

At another historic house, the sound of a child crying is heard coming from the bedroom closet. No one and nothing out of the ordinary is found when the closet is investigated. Recently, documentation was discovered that revealed a small child had been killed when a chimney collapsed.

The sounds of a fife and drum have been heard on High Street. No logical explanation has been found when this happens. Records show that a drummer boy was killed when a Union soldier threw him out the window.

Father Costello's ghost is sometimes seen on the hill behind Saint Peter's Church. This hill is where he often used to go to pray and where he reportedly watched the raid on Harper's Ferry. The church is also haunted. St. Peter's Catholic Church was used as a hospital during the Civil War. A young soldier was brought to the hospital for treatment. He was left outside the hospital until doctors were able to treat him. But his injuries were more severe than anyone realized. The young man died as he crossed the threshold into the church.

Not realizing he was dying, the appreciative soldier uttered "Thank God I'm saved!" Those were his last words. Over the years, some visitors have heard a male voice whispering a few indistinguishable words and some have also claimed to see a strange yellowish light as they enter the church. But it disappears as soon as they are completely inside the old church.

The Iron Horse Restaurant, now abandoned, has a spooky history. Several tenants have moved into the building only to move out quickly as if something scared them off. Rattling and footsteps have been heard by passersby, but the building is vacant. One time, a witness heard a noise that he said sounded like someone was falling down the stairs. When the noise was investigated, no one and nothing out of the usual was found inside the old building. But historical documents show that a Civil War soldier was shot, causing him to fall down the stairs. Maybe this soldier is still here?

Screaming Jenny is another well-known Harper's Ferry ghost. A woman ran from a burning building seeking help only to wind up in the path of an oncoming train. According to legend, the woman lived alone in a tiny wooden shanty near the railroad tracks. While trying to warm herself over an open fire, her skirt caught fire. The rest of her clothes quickly ignited and then she was struck by a train which was passing through town at the exact moment Jenny ran out of the shack. A few witnesses, including train engineers, have reported seeing a ball of light near the railroad tracks.

Dangerfield Newby is another local ghost. He was part of John Brown's raid on Harper's Ferry. He was killed by a resident of the town. According to witnesses, his spirit is sometimes seen in an alley off Main Street. The figure has a scar across his throat and is wearing old clothes, including a hat.

Some claim there are more ghosts than this, such as the ghost of Mrs. Harper and other unknown spirits. But I have not been able to substantiate those stories. One thing is clear. Harper's Ferry is one of the most haunted historic sites in the U.S.

A Ghost Hunter's Guide to the Most Haunted Historic Sites in America

Visitor Information

The park is open daily from 9 a.m. – 5 p.m. There are guided ranger tours daily throughout the year. If going on your own, be sure to visit John Brown's Fort, The Point, Maryland Heights, and Loudoun Heights. The peak season is summer. There are year round living history events.
https://www.nps.gov/hafe/planyourvisit/living-history-events.htm
Ghost tours are given by Ghost Tours of Harpers Ferry.
www.harpersferryghost.20m.com/

Harper's Ferry Park Visitor Center (8 miles east of Charles Town, WV)
171 Shoreline Drive
Harpers Ferry, WV 25425

https://www.nps.gov/hafe/index.htm

Coming from Gettysburg National Military Park (one hour away): Take Rt. 15 south to Frederick, MD. At Frederick, take Rt. 340 South Exit. Follow Rt. 340 to Harpers Ferry.

Coming from Washington, D.C. (one hour away): Get on the beltway, then take I-495 to I-270 N. Follow I-270 to Frederick, MD and take Rt. 340 South Exit to Harpers Ferry.

Harper's Ferry is 20 miles southeast of Frederick, MD and 50 miles from Washington, DC; and 13.5 hours from Orlando, FL (910 miles).

Terrance Zepke

Grand Canyon

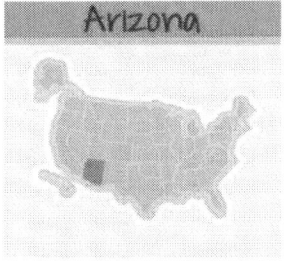

A Ghost Hunter's Guide to the Most Haunted Historic Sites in America

Grand Canyon

FUN FACTS:

The Grand Canyon is haunted by more ghosts than you can count on one hand!

The Grand Canyon National Park is considered to be one of the biggest and best parks in our park system.

There are lots of available activities, such as hiking, ghost walks, railway tours, float trips, helicopter rides, Skywalk, and catching a movie in the Grand Canyon Caverns!

The History

The Grand Canyon is world renown because of its sheer size and beauty. It extends 270 miles with a width of eighteen miles and a depth of one mile. And it dates back more than six million years.

    U.S. government sanctioned expeditions began in the 1800s to explore the canyon. By 1893, it was awarded protection as a federal forest reserve. It became a national park in 1919. It was one of the first parks established by the newly created National Park Service.

    The Grand Canyon National Park, part of the Colorado River Basin, is comprised of more than one million acres. It is one of the most visited parks in America, averaging five million visitors a year. The most popular activities are hiking, camping, rafting, and sightseeing.

    It is inhabited by Native Americans and lots of wildlife. The Pueblos believed the canyon to be a holy site. There are more than 1,500 species of plants here! It is considered to be one of the seven natural wonders of the world.

Grand Canyon National Park Wildlife by the Numbers:

Number of bird species in park: 287
Number of mammal species: 88
Number of reptile and amphibians species: 58
Number of fish species: 26
Endangered wildlife species: 3 (bald eagle, peregrine falcon, humpback chub)

Fun Facts About the Grand Canyon National Park:

Number of known archaeological sites within the park: 2,700
Number of Indian reservations in the park: 1 (Havasupai)
Number of buildings listed as National Landmarks: 120
Number of structures on National Register of Historic Places: 136

 **The Hauntings**

Where to begin? The Grand Canyon is one of the most haunted historic sites in America. Let's start with the two ghosts that haunt the Hopi House.

Hopi House Ghosts

The Hopi House was built on the South Rim in 1904. It was the first of eight projects designed by Architect Mary Colter, who also designed Phantom Ranch, Desert View Watchtower, Bright Angel Lodge, Hermit's Rest, Lookout Studio, Colter Hall, and Victor Hall. It is a gift shop specializing in local Native American arts and crafts. And it is haunted by The Brown Boys.

I haven't been able to find the origin of these ghosts. But their antics are well known. These spirits make their presence known to Hopi House employees in no uncertain terms. Merchandise is often found all over the floor when employees arrive in the morning or dolls are lined up in a particular way (and not the way they were left at closing the previous night). The mischievous spirits also like to run around upstairs at night. If an employee is working late and goes upstairs to investigate the loud footsteps, he never finds anyone. Computers are also found rebooted when employees arrive in the morning, but everything was shut down when the store closed the previous day.

Hopi House

Ghost of Rees Griffiths

The ghost of Rees Griffiths haunts the North Kaibab Trail. He was the foreman in charge of a blasting crew working in the area. He was crushed by a boulder while blasting this trail. His grave is between Phantom Ranch and Black Bridge. He may be gone, but his spirit lingers along this trail. He often makes his presence known to campers and trail crews if they work until dusk or later. A ball of light has been seen hovering over his grave.

Wandering Woman

This is the least seen of all the Grand Canyon ghosts, presumably because she is in the most remote part of the canyon. Only ten percent of visitors go to the North Rim (Most visit the South Rim). Furthermore, she appears in one of the least visited areas of the North Rim. According to legend, she committed suicide in the lodge in the 1920s after learning her husband (and by some accounts her son too) had been killed in a hiking accident. The lodge was destroyed by fire in the 1930s but was rebuilt. Over the years, many employees have seen the Wandering Woman. She is described as wearing a white dress accented with pretty flowers and has a scarf on her head. She often appears in doorways and disappears just as quickly. She has also been seen on the Transept Trail on occasion.

Ghosts of "Crash Canyon"

In 1956, two jets collided over the Grand Canyon, crashing into Chuar Butte and Temple Butte. Due to accessibility issues, it took a special team to recover the bodies of the passengers and crew. They are buried in a mass grave at Yavapai Overlook. Rangers and rafters sometimes see ghosts in this area. They are wearing vintage clothing and seem disoriented. Some are crying or screaming. When approached, they simply vanish. Inexplicable lights have been seen on occasion in an area where there is no camping or trails. Crash Canyon is not accessible. The only way to see it is if you are on the river. Guides will point it out as you pass the area.

El Tovar Lodge was built before the Grand Canyon was officially a park.

El Tovar Ghost

Fred Harvey was the contractor for most of the Grand Canyon development, including the Hopi House and El Tovar Lodge. He is sometimes seen in the hotel wearing a black hat and long, heavy coat. That was the outfit he often wore while walking along the railroad inspecting the job site. There is a woman wearing a 1930s dress that is seen on occasion. A night guard quit and never came back after seeing her one night. Stranger sightings include deathly faces sometimes appearing in the guest room mirrors. One guest paused to check her makeup and left without taking her belongings. She ran downstairs to report the incident and sent an employee to collect her luggage. Employees have reported seeing a ball of light floating across the dining room and exiting out a window facing the canyon. A strange and foul odor has been reported in the service elevator.

Grand Canyon Caverns

Grand Canyon Caverns

A male apparition is often seen at the top and bottom of the elevator shaft which is believed to be the ghost of Walter Peck. The caverns were once used as a burial ground for Native Americans. Their bodies have been removed but the sounds of their burial chanting and singing are still heard by some visitors. Indian spirits have been seen on occasion performing what is believed to be a burial ritual.

Sidebar: Kolb Skeleton

Ellsworth and Emory Kolb built a photography studio on the South Rim in 1904. They were visited by a honeymooning couple, Bessie and Glen Hyde, in 1928. They last saw this couple heading down Bright Angel Trail. Their boat was found the following month on the bank with all their supplies in it, but the couple's bodies were never found. But a skeleton was found when the Kolb's daughter was cleaning out the studio after his death. It is believed to be the skeleton of a miner Emory found near Yavapai Point. His daughter remembers him bringing it out to show guests. The skeleton has a bullet hole in his skull. Did someone murder the miner for his stake? While not ghost related, it is nonetheless an intriguing mystery.

Visitor Information

With close to five million visitors a year, you need to plan your visit carefully, especially in regards to lodging and key attractions, such as the Grand Canyon Skywalk. One of the things that many visitors choose to do is the Skywalk. There is an additional fee, but it is a unique (and a bit scary!) experience.

Permits are required for backcountry camping, river trips, filming, and special events, such as ghost investigations. A popular tourist activity is riding the Grand Canyon Railway, which runs from Williams, AZ to the South Rim of the Grand Canyon. The historic train depot is across the street from the El Tovar Lodge.

Grand Canyon Skywalk

The Grand Canyon is located in the northwest corner of Arizona. The canyon separates the park into two areas: North Rim and South Rim. Most tourists visit the South Rim, which is open all year. Free shuttle buses make getting around easy. South Rim Pocket Guide & Map can be downloaded for free at https://www.nps.gov/grca/learn/news/upload/sr-pocket-map.pdf. The North Rim of the park is more remote than the South Rim. Also, lodging, restaurants, and shops are only open from May 15th through October 15 each year. It is on the Utah side of the Grand Canyon. The North Rim Pocket Guide & Map can be downloaded for free at https://www.nps.gov/grca/learn/news/upload/nr-pocket-map.pdf.
8 South Entrance Road
Grand Canyon Village, AZ 86023

https://www.nps.gov/grca/index.htm

The Grand Canyon is 4.5 hours (276 miles) from Las Vegas, NV; 8.5 hours (522 miles) from Salt Lake City, UT; and 11 hours (677 miles) from Denver, CO.

A Ghost Hunter's Guide to the Most Haunted Historic Sites in America

Empire State Building

Empire State Building

FUN FACTS:

The Empire State Building was the tallest structure in the world when it was built.

It has been haunted since the 1940s.

Many movies, television shows and ads have been filmed here. The most famous was KING KONG, which was released on March 2, 1933.

The History

The Empire State Building is a New York City icon located in midtown Manhattan. It is home to many offices and employees, including dozens of broadcasting stations. New York has been dubbed the Empire State, so that is how this building came by its name.

Known as one of the Seven Wonders of the Modern World, this building has won numerous architectural awards. Built in the architectural style of Art Deco, it is visited by millions of tourists every year. It is owned by the Empire State Realty Trust. Construction began on the skyscraper on March 17, 1930, and the building opened on May 1, 1931. It cost $41 million to build, which is $637 million in today's dollars.

One of the most significant events to occur here was a 1945 airplane crash. William Franklin Smith Jr. was piloting a B-25 Mitchell bomber plane on route to Newark Airport on a routine mission. But it was a foggy day, and he turned right instead of left shortly after passing the Chrysler Building. He managed to avoid a few other skyscrapers before careening into the north side of the Empire State Building. His plane crashed into the building at the 79th floor. The structural damage was not too bad, but the hit resulted in fourteen fatalities (three crewmen and eleven people inside the building).

The Empire State Building is the fifth-tallest building in America behind the One World Trade Center, Willis Tower, 432 Park Avenue, Trump International Hotel and Tower. It is the 25th tallest building in the world. It has been on the National Register of Historic Places since 1982 and has been designated a National Historic Landmark since 1986.

MORE FUN FACTS:

*This building has its own zip code.
*It is 1,860 steps from the street to the 102nd floor.
*There are 6,500 windows in the building.
*There are 73 elevators, including service elevators.

*The building technically has 102 floors with another floor for special use.
*The lobby is four stories high.
*The base measures the equivalent of two acres.

The Hauntings

On May 1, 1947, twenty-three-year-old Evelyn McHale got up and got dressed. She took great care with her appearance that morning. She put on her best dress and heels, a pretty scarf, and a pearl necklace. She made sure her hair and makeup were perfect. She checked her watch and collected her purse and coat, stopping just long enough to dash off a short note.

Evelyn made her way to the Empire State Building where she bought a ticket permitting her access to its observation deck. When she reached the deck, she paused for a moment to appreciate the view. Arguably, the view from the 86th floor of the Empire State Building is one of the best in the city.

Coolly and calmly, Evelyn touched up her lipstick and put it back into her purse. She put the purse down beside her and then removed her coat. She folded it neatly and slid it underneath her pocketbook. Satisfied that she was ready, Even took and deep breath—and jumped.

She landed on the roof of a limousine, which was parked on 33rd Street. Drivers and pedestrians were shocked at the sight. A photography student, Robert Wiley, happened to be near the scene. He raced over to the limo and took a photo. *Life* published this photo in its May 11, 1947 issue. What was most remarkable was how serene the corpse appeared. She looked like a sleeping beauty.

What made this pretty, young woman taking her life? That remains a mystery to this day. Even though Evelyn McHale left a suicide note, it didn't explain things satisfactorily. It most certainly did not make sense to her fiancé, Barry Rhodes.

A Ghost Hunter's Guide to the Most Haunted Historic Sites in America

"I don't think I would make a good wife for anyone. Rhodes will be better off without me. Tell my father, I have too many of my mother's tendencies."

Some speculate that she was just too frightened of the future to face it. Others believe she may have suffered from depression or some other mental illness that may have run in her family. Whatever the motive, the outcome is tragic—and supernatural.

Ever since May 1, 1947, a female spirit has been seen on the observation deck and in the ladies bathroom, touching up her lipstick. Some have even watched the woman jump and then vanish before their very eyes before they can even finish screaming.

Had she not taken her life, McHale was scheduled to marry an ex-soldier named Barry Rhodes just a few weeks later. Rhodes swore she had behaved normally in the hours leading up to her death, giving no indication of the torment she was obviously in. Understandably, he was shocked and devastated by her suicide.

Sadly, McHale is just one of many who have ended their lives jumping off the Empire State Building. That same year, 1947, five other people also jumped to their deaths. A total of thirty people have taken their lives by plummeting to their deaths off the Empire State Building. A fence had to be erected around the outside deck to prevent any more loss of lives. Guards also patrol the observation decks in hopes of thwarting any suicide attempts. There have also been two shootings at or in front of the building.

In addition to seeing a female specter wearing vintage clothes, muffled cries and screams have been heard. With so much sadness and tragedy, is it any wonder this is one of the most haunted historic sites in America?

Observation Deck of Empire State Building

Visitor Information

There are indoor and outdoor observation areas on the 86th floor. There is also an observation deck on the 102nd floor. It was closed in 1999 but has been open since 2005. However, it is sometimes closed on very busy days since it is much smaller than the other decks. It is one of the most popular tourist attractions in New York City. More than 110 million people have visited the Empire State Building. Here are some tips to ensure you have the best experience:

*There are two different fees if you go to both 86th and 102nd-floor observation decks. The best view is from the 86th floor as it affords a 360-degree view of the city.

*Be prepared for long entrance lines—and several of them. There is a sidewalk line, the lobby elevator line, the ticket line, the second elevator line, and the line to get off the elevator and onto the observation deck! If money is no object, there is a ticket you can buy to "Skip the Line!" that catapults you to the front of the line. Just to prepare you mentally, more money is made from ticket sales than from office space rentals throughout the 102-floor building!

A Ghost Hunter's Guide to the Most Haunted Historic Sites in America

*There is a special attraction on the second floor. It is called the NY Sky Ride. It is a simulated aerial tour over the city. This event lasts twenty-five minutes and costs about $40-$60 for children, adults, and seniors.

*You can enhance your visit by getting the free Empire State Building Experience app that is available on Google Play and the App Store.

*The best times are between 8-11 a.m., late afternoon (3-5 p.m.) and between 11 p.m. and 2 a.m.

*Be sure to allow at least an hour for your visit unless you are planning to buy a SKIP THE LINE pass. In addition to the observation decks, there are exhibits, shops, restaurants, and a visitor's center.

*You cannot take the stairs nor do you want to since there are more than 1,500 steps to the top!

*If you are looking for a romantic evening, there is a resident saxophone player who is fantastic. Performances are on the 86th-floor deck Thursdays – Saturdays from sunset until midnight.

*The building and observation decks are open to the public every day year round from 8 a.m. – 2 a.m. The building is on Fifth Avenue between West 33rd and 34th Streets.

350 Fifth Avenue
Manhattan, New York 10118

www.esbnyc.com (website reveals lighting calendar, video of light show, and more)

New York City is 18.5 hours from Kansas City, KS (1201 miles); 3 hours from Baltimore, MD (192 miles); and 8 hours and forty-five minutes from Greensboro, NC (535 miles).

Terrance Zepke

Golden Gate Bridge

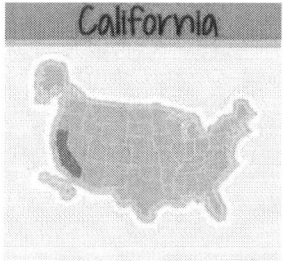

Golden Gate Bridge

FUN FACTS:

The bridge cost $35 million to build in 1937. This is equivalent to $1.7 billion dollars today.

More suicides have taken place on this bridge than any other bridge in the world except for Nanjing Yangtze River Bridge in China.

In addition to being famous for its design, it is well known for its ghosts—and ghost ship!

Terrance Zepke

A virtual bridge tour can be seen at http://goldengate.org/multimedia/index.php.

The History

Construction on the Golden Gate Bridge began in 1933. The bridge opened on May 27, 1937. Situated at the entrance of San Francisco Bay, it extends 1.7 miles. The bridge crosses the Golden Gate Strait (the one-mile-wide by the three-mile-long channel between the Bay and the Pacific Ocean), which is how it came to be called the Golden Gate Bridge.

Ten men died during its construction. Nineteen crew members nearly died but were saved by the extensive safety netting that had been placed under the bridge. The survivors formed a club, the Halfway to Hell Club, to remind themselves how close they came to dying.

The chief engineer of this project, Joseph Strauss, is the main reason they are alive. If not for his meticulous safety precautions, far more lives would have been lost during this dangerous project. There is a statue of him at nearly Golden Gate Pavilion.

The Golden Gate Bridge is a suspension bridge that is not only a famous landmark but also a Wonder of the Modern World. It is also a toll bridge. Since 1968, a one-way toll (southbound) has been collected. This was the first bridge in the world to collect a toll, but now it is a common practice. The toll is waived during the week for vehicles with three or more passengers, buses, and motorcycles from 5:00 a.m. – 9 a.m. and from 4:00 p.m. – 6 p.m. No toll is charged for pedestrians.

Approximately 115,000 vehicles cross this bridge every day. There is enough concrete in the anchorages and piers to pave a sidewalk all the way from San Francisco to New York. It is comprised of 80,000 miles of steel wire. The bridge is ninety-feet wide, and the total weight is 887,000 tons (including bridge, anchorages, and approaches).

So many suicides have occurred that a HELP button has been installed on the bridge.

The Hauntings

The bridge is the site of more tragedy than most of us realize. There is a suicide every two weeks on this bridge. The unofficial number of deaths is 1,300 – 1,600, depending on the source. One of the most well-known suicides was Roy Larson Raymond, who was the founder of Victoria Secret. The suicides became so commonplace that a morbid club was formed in the 1970s. The Suicide Club used to hold a party every time a suicide occurred.

What's interesting is that this isn't the tallest bridge in the area. That honor goes to the San Francisco Oakland Bay Bridge. Many of the men and women who committed suicide crossed the San Franciso Oakland Bay Bridge to reach the Golden Gate Bridge, presumably because it is more renowned. Remarkably, more than two dozen people have survived their suicide attempt.

Loud, lingering screams and anguished cries are often heard, especially on foggy nights. It is commonly believed these are the ghosts of the suicide jumpers. Jumpers descend at a rate of seventy-five miles an hour before crashing into the water.

There is also a ghost ship that is seen on occasion. In 1853, the *SS Tennessee* ran aground in heavy fog in the Golden Gate Strait. The ship was carrying 550 passengers and fourteen chests of gold. All the passengers and gold made it safely to shore before the ship sank to its watery grave.

Or is the ship really gone? Ever since that time, on very foggy nights, a phantom ship has been seen on occasion by another ship. No crew or passengers are seen on deck, and the ship does not show up on radar. Before the other ship can get a closer look, the phantom ship disappears into the fog.

Known as advection fog, this type of fog is typically close to the ground. It happens when the warm air from the Pacific Ocean meets the cool California coast air. This event is not uncommon in coastal areas, but what is unique is the role the bridge plays in regards to the fog. The Golden Gate Bridge "pushes" the fog up or down around the bridge, according to the wind factor. It was painted bright orange in large part because of the fog. Even during a dense fog, the bridge is usually visible due to its vivid color.

Visitor Information

The Golden Gate Bridge Visitor Plaza at the southeast side of the bridge. The Bridge Welcome Center orients visitors and houses exhibits. It is open 9 am to 6 pm. There is a snack bar and a café. To access the Visitor Plaza when traveling northbound, take the last San Francisco northbound exit from Highway 101. When traveling southbound on Highway 101, proceed through lane #1 (far right, west side) of the Toll Plaza and take the first exit onto Merchant Road. Make the first right turn and proceed down a small hill to the stop sign. Make another right turn on to the tunnel roadway that passes underneath the Toll Plaza. This road takes visitors to the southeast parking lot. Parking is very limited at the Golden Gate Bridge and alternative methods of accessing the Bridge Visitor Plaza is recommended, such as a bicycle, public transit, rideshare, taxi, tour bus, and car service.

San Francisco is famous for its cable cars.

There is no physical (street) address for the Golden Gate Bridge. For more tourist information visit http://www.goldengatebridge.com/.

San Francisco is 1.5 hours (88 miles) from Sacramento, CA; 20.5 hours (1,414 miles) from Rapid City, SD; and 48 minutes (50 miles) from San Jose, CA.

A Ghost Hunter's Guide to the Most Haunted Historic Sites in America

Wrigley Field

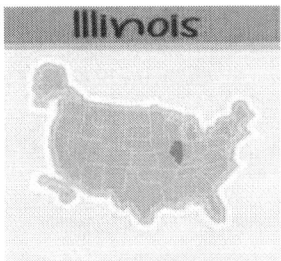

Wrigley Field

FUN FACTS:

Even though the stadium opened in 1914, it was 1937 before a scoreboard was installed.

This ballpark is one of the few in America that is both historic and haunted.

Visitors can take an insider's walking tour of the ballpark that reveals parts of the park that are normally off limits to the public and learn fascinating facts, such as the Cubs were the first MLB team to let fans keep foul balls.

A Ghost Hunter's Guide to the Most Haunted Historic Sites in America

TIMELINE

1914—The ballpark opened on April 23, 1914 as the home of the Chicago Whales. It cost $500,000 to build, which is roughly equivalent to $15 million in 2016 dollars. It was the site of a Lutheran Seminary before it was ballpark.

1915—The Federal League folded, and that was the end of the Chicago Whales. The Cubs were bought by several businessmen, including William Wrigley. The men moved the Cubs from the West Side to this ballpark on the North Side.

1921—William Wrigley bought the ballpark, which was known as Cubs Park.

1932—The ballpark was renamed Wrigley Field in 1932 to honor team owner, William Wrigley, who passed away that year.

1937—A scoreboard was added. FYI: No baseball has ever hit the scoreboard, but plenty of parked cars have been dinged.

1988—Lights were installed. The Cubs were the first team to play night games.

2009—Tribune Company sold the Cubs to Thomas S. Ricketts. Tribune had owned the team since 1981 when they bought it for $20 million from William Wrigley.

2012—A party patio was added.

2014-2017—A Jumbotron was added, and a major bleacher expansion was completed.

Fun Trivia

Wrigley Field was the first ballpark to have permanent concession stands.

The Cubs haven't won the World Series since 1945 when Charlie Grimm was the team manager.

Nicknames include The Cubbies, the North Siders, the North Side Nine, the Boys in Blue, the Lovable Losers, the Little Bears, and the Blue Bears.

The Cubs were the first baseball team to let fans keep foul balls.

The stadium is state-of-the-art with a restaurant, food deck, and 63 private boxes.

Wrigley Field is the second-oldest major league baseball stadium in the United States (Fenway Park, Boston is the oldest). Wrigley has a seating capacity of 41,160.

2016 was the 100th season of the Chicago Cubs. Happy Anniversary!

# The Hauntings

The most common paranormal activity involves the bullpen. Security guards often report that the phone in the bullpen rings in the middle of the night. But that is a direct line to the dugout, which means that someone would have to be in the dugout making the call for it to ring in the bullpen. The guards always check the dugout upon hearing the ringing phone. It is always empty, which is logical since it is the middle of the night and the ballpark is closed and empty except for the guards. The dugout cannot be called from any other phone line but the bullpen.

Dugout=sunken area adjacent to the field where a team's bench is located. There is one dugout near each foul line between home plate and first or third base. Typically, the home tea has the first base dugout. There is a telephone so that the manager or pitching coach can communicate with the bullpen.

Bullpen=an area on the field or separated from the field by a fence where relief pitchers go to warm up before going into the game

Many believe that the caller is the ghost of Charlie Grimm, who was the Cubs manager in the 1930s and 1940s. His calls to the bullpen to make last minute pitching changes were well known. Security guards have seen Grimm roaming the hallways. He sometimes greets the guards before disappearing! That's not surprisingly because Grimm loved the Cubs. That's why he was buried in left field, at least according to legend. Neither the Cubs nor the Grimms' family has commented on this story. Some believe the spirit of Charlie Grimm will never leave until the Cubs win the World Series again, which they haven't done since he was their manager.

Chicago broadcaster, Harry Caray, may be keeping Grimm company at Wrigley Field. Even though he died in 1998, fans still claim to see Caray on occasion sitting in the press box or in the outfield bleachers, still cheering on his beloved Cubs.

Rounding out this trio of ghosts if Steve Goodman, who was a diehard fan and songwriter. He wrote their anthem, "Go Cubs, Go!" Fans and players often say they've seen him sitting behind the batter's box. This seems unlikely given that he's been dead since 1984. But he may still be attending games, at least in spirit. His ashes are buried underneath home plate, so maybe he is just sticking close to "home."

When the Tribune Company owned the Chicago Cubs, they brought in paranormal researchers to prove or disapprove paranormal activity. Chicago Hauntings conducted a thorough investigation and discovered unexplainable cold spots in some of the offices and outfield bleachers. They also reported abnormal EVPS and EMFs. However, they didn't find anything unusual in the broadcasting booth.

THE CURSE OF THE BILLY GOAT!

Sidebar: This is a well-known tale in the major league baseball world. The owner of Billy Goat Tavern, Billy, Sianis, bought two tickets to Game #4 of the 1945 World Series (Cubs vs. Detroit Tigers) for him and his pet goat, Murphy. When he arrived at the stadium, he was told he could enter but not his goat as no animals are allowed in the park. Sianis did not take the news well.

He had brought the goat to bring "good luck" to his beloved Cubs and this was how they were treated!

Furious, he reportedly placed a curse on the team. *"Them Cubs, they ain't gonna win no more!"* Sianis yelled as he departed.

In 1969, Sianis claimed he had lifted the curse before he died that same year. In 1973, his nephew, Sam, brought the goat to Wrigley to try to end the curse once and for all. The goat, a descendent of Murphy, was transported by limo to the ballfield where he arrived wearing a sign *"All is forgiven. Let me lead the Cubs to the pennant."* However, ushers again denied entry to the goat due to their no animals in the stadium policy. Maybe they should have just made an exception to their policy. Or maybe we shouldn't give any weight to this silly story. Maybe it is just bad luck—a very long losing streak? The Cubs don't think so. This curse has been taken so seriously that owners have tried all kinds of tactics over the years to get rid of the curse, including Greek Orthodox Priest spraying holy water in the dugout, a blessing on the ballpark by priests, and "Crack the Curse" and "Reverse the Curse" Campaigns. Since the Cubs have not won a World Series since 1908 or even played in one since 1945, it seems none of these efforts have been successful. With the Cubs playing well so far this season, perhaps soon after this book is published, the curse will finally end? http://www.billygoattavern.com/legend/curse/.

Visitor Information

The Cubs offer insider tours of the ballpark. www.chicago.cubs.mlb.com. There are also some private companies that offer walking tours outside of the stadium. www.historyofwrigley.com.

1060 W. Addison Street

Chicago, IL 60613

www.chicago.cubs.mlb.com

Chicago is 12 hours (790 miles) from New York City; 1.5 hours (92 miles) from Milwaukee, WI; and 11.5 hours (760 miles) from Philadelphia, PA.

Terrance Zepke

King's Arms Tavern

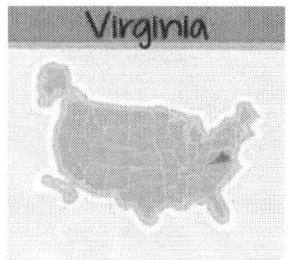

King's Arms Tavern

FUN FACTS:

This tavern has been operating continuously since 1772.

In colonial times, if a town didn't have at least one tavern, they had to pay a fine.

The tavern is haunted by a former employee who is still performing her duties to this day.

The History

On February 6, 1772, this advertisement appeared in the Virginia Gazette:

I have just opened TAVERN opposite Raleigh at the sign of the KING'S ARMS...and shall be much obliged to the Gentlemen who favour me with their company.

The ad was placed by the tavern owner, Jane Vobe, who ran several taverns in the Williamsburg area. During colonial times, a tavern was vitally important to travelers. It was a bar, restaurant, and inn all in one. News was disseminated to and through fellow travelers. A weary traveler could get a hot meal and lodging for the night. Or a traveler could take a short break and grab a sandwich and glass of ale before continuing his journey. Some even doubled as banks, general stores, and post offices.

Taverns were considered so necessary that the government levvied a fine on any town that didn't have one. The first tavern in America opened in Boston in March 1634. The first one in Virginia, Hanover Tavern, opened in 1733. King's Arms Tavern catered to an upscale clientele which included government officials and politicians. A couple of her more renowned customers were George Washington and Thomas Jefferson.

Today, the tavern is part of historic Colonial Williamsburg, which is a living history museum comprised of the historic district of Williamsburg, Virginia. This historical site is made up of 300 acres of buildings. Many of these structures are reportedly haunted.

This Tavern still serves the same kind of fare as Mrs. Vobe did, such as Game Pye, Peanut Soupe, and Prime Rib. Here is their specialty:

Mrs. Vobe's Tavern Dinner Choice of Soupe followed by Sage and Rosemary rubbed half of Cornish Hen, blended Wild Rice Dressing, Scuppernong-chutney Sauce and Cook Vegetables ending sweetly with choice of Williamsburg Ice Cream or Pecan Pie $35.95

The Hauntings

Irma is the resident ghost of King's Arms Tavern. According to most sources, she was a tavern employee in the 1700s who died when a dropped candle caused a fire. However, that story is just a legend. According to tavern employees, Irma lived in one of the upstairs rooms, which is now one of the tavern's dining rooms. She was the tavern manager, but there was no fire. Irma died of a heart attack in the early 1950s.

Most employees have had encounters with Irma, who they believe watches over the place. Some claim to feel her presence when they are in this dining room, which is known as the Up Room. Irma often blows out candles and turns off lights when it is closing time. The staff has witnessed candles and lights going out as if blown out or turned off by an invisible presence. It is also interesting to note that neither the lights or candles go out except at or near closing time.

During the Christmas holiday season, Colonial Williamsburg is decorated with lots of greenery, lanterns, and electric (candle) lights. The electric candles are placed in all the front windows of the tavern. Employees are responsible for extinguishing these lights at closing time by unscrewing the little light bulb. No matter how many times and employees confirm the lights are off, they are found "on" when the manager arrives the next morning. Employees have noted the extinguished lights from the street as they head home after their shift, only to learn the lights were on the next morning.

Irma is so well known and regarded by employees of the tavern that most of them say *"Goodnight, Irma!"* as they leave for the night. This has become a tradition, and some even think it is good luck.

There are plenty more haunted buildings in Colonial Williamsburg. Wyeth House is haunted by Lady Skipwith. Chownings Tavern is haunted by an unknown man and some sorority spirits. Peyton Randolph House is haunted by a child spirit. The College of William & Mary is haunted by Civil War and Revolutionary War ghosts.

A ghost tour of Colonial Williamsburg is offered year round, and there is candlelit storytelling seasonally.
www.colonialwilliamsburg.com/plan/calendar/ghosts-amoungst-us/

Visitor Information

Lunch and dinner are served every day except on Tuesdays and Wednesdays. Special seasonal events and menus are offered. The tavern is not handicapped accessible.

For the best chance of an Irma encounter, you should have a late dinner and sit in the Up Room.

416 E. Duke of Gloucester Street
Williamsburg, VA 23185

https://www.colonialwilliamsburg.com/do/restaurants/historic-dining-taverns/kings-arms/

Colonial Williamsburg Visitor Center

101 Visitor Center Drive

Williamsburg, VA 23185

www.colonialwilliamsburg.com

Williamsburg is three hours (210 miles) from Raleigh, NC; 2.5 hours (154 miles) from Washington, DC; and 10 hours (677 miles) from St. Augustine, FL.

Terrance Zepke

Hollywood Sign

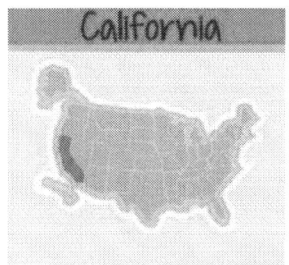

A Ghost Hunter's Guide to the Most Haunted Historic Sites in America

Hollywood Sign

Photo taken by Thomas Wolf

FUN FACTS:

Originally, the sign that overlooks the Hollywood Hills was "HOLLYWOODLAND."

The HOLLYWOODLAND sign was originally built in 1923 at the cost of $21,000 and was meant to last a year.

It is the only sign in the world (that I know of) that is haunted.

Original sign

The History

The first movie made in Hollywood was a seventeen-minute "short" called *In Old California*. It was released in 1910. And so the legendary Hollywood was born. But this sign is more than a landmark. It is an iconic symbol of the American dream. Thousands of men and women have descended on Hollywood over the years. All come with the dream of making it "big" as an actor or actress.

The sign was erected in 1923, ironically not as a symbol or landmark. Its purpose was to advertise an upscale real estate development. The $21,000 sign was only meant to be temporary, like a billboard. It originally read "Hollywoodland." Tractors and teams of mules were used to haul the panels up the mountain. The panels were crafted into letters and secured using wires, pipes, and telephone poles. To light up the sign, four thousand 20-watt light bulbs are strategically positioned onto the thirteen letters. It was anticipated that the sign would last about a year. However, no one anticipated the attention it would garner. For nearly a decade, its notoriety and popularity grew by leaps and bounds. It was featured in movies and became an L.A. tourist attraction.

And then the sign became infamous when a young actress committed suicide by flinging herself off the top of the sign (read more about this in The Hauntings later in this chapter).

By the 1940s, the sign was in bad shape due to a natural deterioration. Locals wanted the eyesore removed. The developers relinquished the sign to the City of Los Angeles. In partnership with the Hollywood Chamber of Commerce, the sign was restored with the last four letters being dropped. To thwart vandalism, a security system was installed and is monitored 24/7 by City of Los Angeles security specialists.

Located on Mount Lee in the Hollywood Hills area of the Santa Monica Mountains (Griffith Park), the sign overlooks Hollywood and Los Angeles. It was declared a Historical Landmark in 1973. Over the years, celebrities have contributed to the expensive maintenance and upkeep of this sign, ranging from Gloria Swanson to Hugh Hefner.

By the 1970s, the sign had deteriorated to this state.

Fun Facts about the Sign:

*The letters are all white and all capital, extending 45-feet-high and 350-feet-wide.
*The sign is under the guardianship of The Trust for Public Land.
*The sign is often seen in ads, television shows, and movies.
*The sign was demolished in 1978 so that a new and improved sign could be built.
*There was no "Hollywood" sign for more than three months while the new sign was built and erected, including an elaborate steel frame to support the huge letters. Nearly 200 tons of concrete was used to anchor the sign.
*Helicopters were used to position the massive steel frame.
*The sign you see today is four stories high and 450-feet long. Collectively, it weighs 480,000 pounds. The letters are made of corrugated baked enamel.
*The new sign was unveiled to a television audience of 60 million on the 75th anniversary of Hollywood celebration in November 1978.
*It underwent another major renovation in 2005.

To Be Exact:

H	45 ft. high by 33 ft. 6 inches wide
O	45 ft. high by 33 ft. wide
L	45 ft. high by 31 ft. wide
L	45 ft. high by 31 ft. wide
Y	45 ft. high by 35 ft. wide
W	45 ft. high by 39 ft. 9 inches wide
O	45 ft. high by 33 ft. wide
O	45 ft. high by 33 ft. wide
D	45 ft. high by 33 ft. wide

Back side of sign

The Hauntings

This story begins with an actress named Millicent Lillian (Peg) Entwistle, who may not have achieved the stardom she desired while she was alive, but who immortalized herself on September 18, 1932.

Peg was no stranger to tragedy. Her mother died when she was a child and her father was killed in a car accident just a few years later. Her brothers were sent to live with an uncle in California. Peg stayed in New York, alone but determined to become an actress. She began her studies in her teens. By the time she turned eighteen, Peg was acting in productions with Bette Davis, Dorothy Gish, and Laurette Taylor.

She was married by her nineteenth birthday to actor Robert Keith. The marriage failed and Peg moved on to Los Angeles in 1932. She in the play, *The Mad Hopes*, which also starred Humphrey Bogart. She landed a plum role in *Thirteen Women*. However, poor reviews resulted in most of her scenes being cut and the studio dropping her contract. With her career in a downward spiral, Peg grew depressed. Having already experienced so much sadness in her life and now her big dreams and plans fading away, she had a hard time battling her demons.

Peg began drinking heavily, which did nothing to help her mental state. It probably made her feel all the more hopeless and helpless. After a long night of imbibing, Peg made a reckless and irreversible decision.

She dashed off a quick note before climbing up the trail to the "Hollywood" sign and looking out over the Hollywood Hills. Next, she took off her coat and laid it down beside her purse. Peg then climbed up the maintenance ladder attached to the back side of the first letter "H". Peg paused only momentarily before letting go and plunging to her death. She was barely twenty-four years old.

Her body was discovered two days later by a hiker. Not wanting to get involved, the hiker left an anonymous note and the items he'd found: Peg's coat, purse, and suicide note on the front steps of the Hollywood Police Station. The police recovered the body, but her spirit is still seen to this day.

The ghost is always seen near the sign. She is a pretty, young blond wearing a 1930s dress and short heels. Witnesses describe the spirit as sad and note that she seems to glide or float rather than walk, but seems disoriented. Whenever park rangers, hikers, or joggers approach the young woman to see if she needs assistance, she vanishes.

Park rangers say the best chance of seeing Peg's ghost is late at night when there is fog. The smell of gardenias is sometimes strong right after the ghost is seen. Peg wore a gardenia cologne so that contributes to the theory that she is the ghost that haunts the Hollywood sign. Also, the description given by witnesses describes Peg to a tee.

Some wonder why Peg chose this spot to end her life, but I think the answer is obvious. This sign is a symbol of Hollywood and all the hopes and dreams of those who come here to succeed. For Peg Entwistle, the Hollywood sign was most likely a constant reminder of her failed hopes and dreams. For that reason, it was the perfect place to end her life.

Peg Entwistle

Peg's Suicide Note: *I am afraid. I am a coward. I am sorry for everything. If I had done this a long time ago, it would have saved a lot of pain." P.E.*

Visitor Information

There are three trails that lead to the sign: Mt. Hollywood Trail (easy), Canyon Boulevard Trail (moderate), and Cahuenga Peak Trail (difficult). These trails are open during daylight hours, from sunrise to sunset, year-round. The sign is located on the south side of Mount Lee in Griffith Park, which is north of Mulholland Highway and south of Forest Lawn Memorial Park. There is a barrier and a security system to prevent trespassing. Trespassers are arrested and will receive a one-year probation. A $1,000 fine is also imposed.

Another option is to take a shuttle. For hours of operation and more about this option:

http://hollywoodsign.org/hollywood-sign-schedule-schedule/

There is no physical address for this sign but here are the coordinates:

34°08′02.56″N 118°19′18.00″W 34.1340444°N 118.3216667°W at a 1,578-foot (481 m) elevation.

Los Angeles is two hours (121 miles) from San Diego, CA; 28.5 hours (2,008 miles) from Nashville, TN; and 12 hours (849 miles) from Santa Fe, NM.

http://hollywoodsign.org/

Resources

National Historic Landmarks (NHLs) are nationally significant historic places designated by the Secretary of the Interior because they possess exceptional value or quality in illustrating or interpreting the heritage of the United States. Today, just over 2,500 historic places bear this national distinction. Working with citizens throughout the nation, the National Historic Landmarks Program draws upon the expertise of National Park Service staff who guide the nomination process for new Landmarks and provide assistance to existing Landmarks. www.nps.gov/nhl/

FYI: The states with the most NHLs are California, Illinois, Massachusetts, New York, and Virginia. The states with the least are North Dakota and Nevada.

The **National Register of Historic Places** is the official list of the Nation's historic places worthy of preservation. Authorized by the National Historic Preservation Act of 1966, the National Park Service's National Register of Historic Places is part of a national program to coordinate and support public and private efforts to identify, evaluate, and protect America's historical and archeological resources. www.nps.gov/nr/

The **National Trust for Historic Preservation** is a privately funded non-profit group that protects America's significant (historic) places representing our diverse cultural experience by taking direct action and inspiring broad public support. www.savingplaces.org

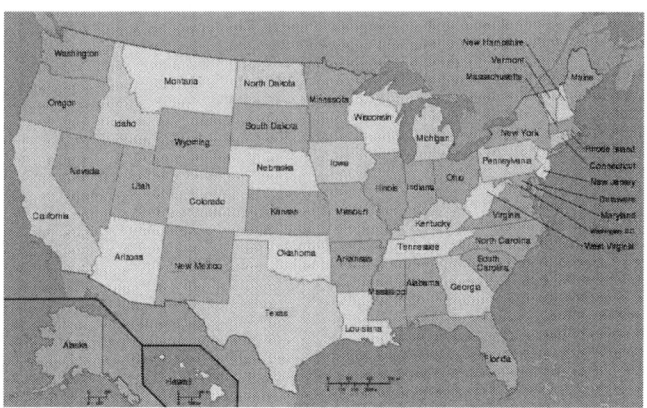

*FYI: The states with the most historic places are **Ohio, Virginia, Pennsylvania, Texas,** and **Kentucky**. A complete list of these historic places can be found at https://en.wikipedia.org/wiki/United_States_National_Register_of_Historic_Places_listings*

Historic Hotels of America is the official program of the **National Trust for Historic Preservation** for recognizing and celebrating the finest Historic Hotels. Historic Hotels of America was founded in 1989. Today, Historic Hotels of America has 275 historic hotels. These historic hotels have all faithfully maintained their authenticity, sense of place, and architectural integrity in the United States of America, the U.S. Virgin Islands, and Puerto Rico. A hotel must be at least fifty years old and designated by the U.S. Secretary of the Interior as a National Historic Landmark or on the National Register of Historic Places. www.historichotels.org

FYI: Concord's Colonial Inn in Concord, Massachusetts is the oldest hotel in America (1716), dating back more than 300 years! http://www.concordscolonialinn.com/

The **National Park Service (NPS)** is an agency of the United States federal government that manages all U.S. national parks, many American national monuments, and other historical properties. It was established on August 25, 1916, by Congress and is an agency of the United States Department of the Interior. www.nps.gov/

FYI: The five most popular national parks are the Great Smokies, Grand Canyon, Yellowstone, Yosemite, and Zion.

A **National Historic Site** (NHS) is a protected place of national historic significance. It is not the same as a National Historical Park (NHP). However, both as managed by the NPS and listed on the National Register of Historic Places. Many are also considered to be National Historic Landmarks.

A **National Heritage Area** (a.k.a. National Heritage Corridor) is a site designated by the U.S. government (Congress) to be worthy of historic preservation.

To find lodging at any park:

https://www.nationalparkreservations.com/

https://www.usparklodging.com/

Fun Quiz

1. The Hollywood sign once had a different name. True or False?
2. Which former president's ghost is most often seen in the White House?
3. King's Arms Tavern is haunted by a Revolutionary War soldier. True or false?
4. Where is Wrigley Field and what baseball team plays there?
5. The most haunted area of Alcatraz is the hospital ward. True or False?
6. There are three haunted rooms in the White House. True or False?
7. Mammoth Cave is haunted by miners. True or False?
8. What tragic event is associated with the Empire State Building and subsequent paranormal activity?
9. The most haunted area of Gettysburg Battlefield is Soldier's Rest. True or False?
10. Who is the most famous ghost seen at the Alamo (hint: he fought in the Battle of the Alamo)?

Quiz Answers: 1. True. The original sign read "Hollywoodland"; 2. Abraham Lincoln; 3. False. It is haunted by a former employee who died in an upstairs room; 4. Chicago Cubs; 5. False. The most haunted area is Cellblock D; 6. False. There are ten haunted rooms; 7. False. The cave is haunted by several spirits including former guides and TB patients but no miners; 8. Evelyn McHale committed suicide by jumping from the top of the building in 1947, and many believe her ghost is still here; 9. False. The most haunted area is Devil's Den; 10. Davy Crockett.

Dear Reader,

Thank you for buying or borrowing *A Ghost Hunter's Guide to the Most Haunted Historic Sites in America*. I hope you enjoyed it—and learned a lot.

I spent a great deal of time compiling this information into what I believe is an easy-to-read, useful reference. I would love to hear from you if you'd like to post a comment on www.terrancezepke.com. I do respond to all comments. If you'd like to learn more about hauntings and receive a FREE "Fifty Fun Facts About Ghosts" report, be sure to sign up for my *Mostly Ghostly* blog.

I would also like to ask you to please share your feedback about this book on Amazon or Goodreads so that other readers might discover this title too.

Authors appreciate readers more than you realize, and we dearly love and depend upon good reviews. If you've never posted a review before, it is easy to do—just tell folks what you liked about this book and why you (hopefully) recommend it: http://www.amazon.com/Terrance-Zepke/e/B000APJNIA/.

Thank you again for your interest in this book. If you enjoyed it, you may want to check out more books in my MOST HAUNTED and SPOOKIEST series.

Terrance

A Ghost Hunter's Guide to the Most Haunted Historic Sites in America

TERRANCE ZEPKE
Series Reading Order & Guide

Terrance Zepke

Series List

Most Haunted Series
Terrance Talks Travel Series
Cheap Travel Series
Spookiest Series
Stop Talking Series
Carolinas for Kids Series
Ghosts of the Carolinas Series
Books & Guides for the Carolinas Series
& More Books by Terrance Zepke

≈

A Ghost Hunter's Guide to the Most Haunted Historic Sites in America

Introduction

Here is a list of titles by Terrance Zepke. They are presented in chronological order although they do not need to be read in any particular order.

Also included is an author bio, a personal message from Terrance, and some other information you may find helpful.

All books are available as digital and print books. They can be found on Amazon, Barnes and Noble, Kobo, Apple iBooks, GooglePlay, Smashwords, or through your favorite independent bookseller.

For more about this author and her books visit her Author Page at: http://www.amazon.com/Terrance-Zepke/e/B000APJNIA/.

You can also connect with Terrance on Twitter **@terrancezepke** or on

www.facebook.com/terrancezepke
www.pinterest.com/terrancezepke
www.goodreads.com/terrancezepke

Sign up for weekly email notifications of the *Terrance Talks Travel* blog to be the first to learn about new episodes of her travel show, cheap travel tips, free downloadable TRAVEL REPORTS, and discover her TRIP PICK OF THE WEEK at www.terrancetalkstravel.com or sign up for her *Mostly Ghostly* blog at www.terrancezepke.com.

≈

Terrance Zepke

TERRANCE TALKS TRAVEL
Podcast

You can follow her travel show, **TERRANCE TALKS TRAVEL: ÜBER ADVENTURES on** www.blogtalkradio.com/terrancetalkstravel or subscribe to it at **iTunes.**

Warning: Listening to this show could lead to a spectacular South African safari, hot-air ballooning over the Swiss Alps, Disney Adventures, and Tornado Tours!

≈

Terrance Zepke is co-host of the writing show, **A WRITER'S JOURNEY: FROM BLANK PAGE TO PUBLISHED.** All episodes can be found on **iTunes** or on www.terrancezepke.com.

≈

AUTHOR BIO

Terrance Zepke studied Journalism at the University of Tennessee and later received a Master's degree in Mass Communications from the University of South Carolina. She studied parapsychology at the renowned Rhine Research Center.

Zepke spends much of her time happily traveling around the world but always returns home to the Carolinas where she lives part-time in both states. She has written hundreds of articles and more than fifty books. She is the host of *Terrance Talks Travel: Über Adventures* and co-host of *A Writer's Journey: From Blank Page to Published*. Additionally, this award-winning and best-selling author has been featured in many publications and programs, such as NPR, CNN, *The Washington Post,* Associated Press, Travel with Rick Steves, Around the World, *Publishers Weekly,* World Travel & Dining with Pierre Wolfe, *San Francisco Chronicle,* Good Morning Show, *Detroit Free Press*, The Learning Channel, and The Travel Channel.

When she's not investigating haunted places, searching for pirate treasure, or climbing lighthouses, she is most likely packing for her next adventure to some far flung place, such as Reykjavik or Kwazulu Natal. Some of her favorite adventures include piranha fishing on the Amazon, shark cage diving in South Africa, hiking the Andes Mountains Inca Trail, camping in the Himalayas, dog-sledding in the Arctic Circle, and a gorilla safari in the Congo.

≈

A Ghost Hunter's Guide to the Most Haunted Historic Sites in America

MOST HAUNTED SERIES

A Ghost Hunter's Guide to the Most Haunted Places in America (2012)
https://read.amazon.com/kp/embed?asin=B0085SG22O&preview=newtab&linkCode=kpe&ref_=cm_sw_r_kb_dp_zerQwb1AMJ0R4

A Ghost Hunter's Guide to the Most Haunted Houses in America (2013)
https://read.amazon.com/kp/embed?asin=B00C3PUMGC&preview=newtab&linkCode=kpe&ref_=cm_sw_r_kb_dp_BfrQwb1WF1Y6T

A Ghost Hunter's Guide to the Most Haunted Hotels & Inns in America (2014)
https://read.amazon.com/kp/embed?asin=B00C3PUMGC&preview=newtab&linkCode=kpe

A Ghost Hunter's Guide to the Most Haunted Historic Sites in America (2016)
https://www.amazon.com/Ghost-Hunters-Haunted-Historic-America-ebook/dp/B01LXADK90/ref=sr_1_1?s=books&ie=UTF8&qid=1475973918&sr=1-1&keywords=a+ghost+hunter%27s+guide+to+the+most+haunted+historic+sites+in+america

The Ghost Hunter's MOST HAUNTED Box Set (3 in 1): Discover America's Most Haunted Destinations (2016)
https://read.amazon.com/kp/embed?asin=B01HISAAJM&preview=newtab&linkCode=kpe&ref_=cm_sw_r_kb_dp_ulz-xbNKND7VT

MOST HAUNTED and SPOOKIEST Sampler Box Set: Featuring *A GHOST HUNTER'S GUIDE TO THE MOST HAUNTED PLACES IN AMERICA* and *SPOOKIEST CEMETERIES* (2017)
https://read.amazon.com/kp/embed?asin=B01N17EEOM&preview=newtab&linkCode=kpe&ref_=cm_sw_r_kb_dp_JFLybCTN3QEF

≈

Terrance Zepke

TERRANCE TALKS TRAVEL SERIES

Terrance Talks Travel: A Pocket Guide to South Africa (2015)
https://read.amazon.com/kp/embed?asin=B00PSTFTLI&preview=newtab&linkCode=kpe&ref_=cm_sw_r_kb_dp_pirQwb12XZX65

Terrance Talks Travel: A Pocket Guide to African Safaris (2015)
https://read.amazon.com/kp/embed?asin=B00PSTFZSA&preview=newtab&linkCode=kpe&ref_=cm_sw_r_kb_dp_jhrQwb0P8Z87G

Terrance Talks Travel: A Pocket Guide to Adventure Travel (2015)
https://read.amazon.com/kp/embed?asin=B00UKMAVQG&preview=newtab&linkCode=kpe&ref_=cm_sw_r_kb_dp_ThrQwb1PVVZAZ

Terrance Talks Travel: A Pocket Guide to Florida Keys (including Key West & The Everglades) (2016)
http://www.amazon.com/Terrance-Talks-Travel-Including-Everglades-ebook/dp/B01EWHML58/ref=sr_1_1?s=books&ie=UTF8&qid=1461897775&sr=1-1&keywords=terrance+talks+travel%3A+a+pocket+guide+to+the+florida+keys

Terrance Talks Travel: The Quirky Tourist Guide to Key West (2017)
https://www.amazon.com/Terrance-Zepke/e/B000APJNIA/ref=sr_ntt_srch_lnk_1?qid=1485052308&sr=8-1

Terrance Talks Travel: The Quirky Tourist Guide to Cape Town (2017)
https://www.amazon.com/Terrance-Zepke/e/B000APJNIA/ref=sr_ntt_srch_lnk_1?qid=1485052308&sr=8-1

Terrance Talks Travel: The Quirky Tourist Guide to Reykjavik (2017)
https://www.amazon.com/Terrance-Zepke/e/B000APJNIA/ref=sr_ntt_srch_lnk_15?qid=1488514258&sr=8-15

Terrance Talks Travel: The Quirky Tourist Guide to Charleston, South Carolina (2017)
https://www.amazon.com/Terrance-Zepke/e/B000APJNIA/ref=sr_ntt_srch_lnk_15?qid=1488514258&sr=8-15

Terrance Talks Travel: The Quirky Tourist Guide to Ushuaia (2017)
https://www.amazon.com/Terrance-Zepke/e/B000APJNIA/ref=sr_ntt_srch_lnk_15?qid=1488514258&sr=8-15

Terrance Talks Travel: The Quirky Tourist Guide to Antarctica (2017)
https://www.amazon.com/Terrance-Zepke/e/B000APJNIA/ref=sr_ntt_srch_lnk_1?qid=1489092624&sr=8-1

A Ghost Hunter's Guide to the Most Haunted Historic Sites in America

TERRANCE TALKS TRAVEL: The Quirky Tourist Guide to Machu Picchu & Cuzco (Peru) 2017
https://read.amazon.com/kp/embed?asin=B07147HLQY&preview=newtab&linkCode=kpe&ref_=cm_sw_r_kb_dp_HmZmzb9FT5E0P

African Safari Box Set: Featuring TERRANCE TALKS TRAVEL: *A Pocket Guide to South Africa* and *TERRANCE TALKS TRAVEL: A Pocket Guide to African Safaris* (2017)
https://read.amazon.com/kp/embed?asin=B01MUH6VJU&preview=newtab&linkCode=kpe&ref_=cm_sw_r_kb_dp_xLFLybAQKFA0B

≈

Terrance Zepke

CHEAP TRAVEL SERIES

How to Cruise Cheap! (2017)
https://www.amazon.com/Cruise-Cheap-CHEAP-TRAVEL-Book-ebook/dp/B01N6NYM1N/

How to Fly Cheap! (2017)
https://www.amazon.com/How-Cheap-CHEAP-TRAVEL-Book-ebook/dp/B01N7Q81YG/

How to Travel Cheap! (2017)
https://read.amazon.com/kp/embed?asin=B01N7Q81YG&preview=newtab&linkCode=kpe&ref_=cm_sw_r_kb_dp_j78KybJVSCXDX

How to Travel FREE or Get Paid to Travel! (2017)
https://read.amazon.com/kp/embed?asin=B01N7Q81YG&preview=newtab&linkCode=kpe&ref_=cm_sw_r_kb_dp_j78KybJVSCXDX

CHEAP TRAVEL SERIES (4 IN 1) BOX SET (2017)
https://read.amazon.com/kp/embed?asin=B071ZGV1TY&preview=newtab&linkCode=kpe&ref_=cm_sw_r_kb_dp_rlZmzbSPV8KG9

A Ghost Hunter's Guide to the Most Haunted Historic Sites in America

SPOOKIEST SERIES

Spookiest Lighthouses (2013)
https://read.amazon.com/kp/embed?asin=B00EAAQA2S&preview

Spookiest Battlefields (2015)
https://read.amazon.com/kp/embed?asin=B00XUSWS3G&preview=newtab&linkCode=kpe&ref=cm_sw_r_kb_dp_okrQwb0TR9F8M

Spookiest Cemeteries (2016)
http://www.amazon.com/Terrance-Zepke/e/B000APJNIA/ref=sr_ntt_srch_lnk_1?qid=1457641303&sr=8-1

Spookiest Objects (2017)
https://read.amazon.com/kp/embed?asin=B0728FMVZF&preview=newtab&linkCode=kpe&ref=cm_sw_r_kb_dp_eqZmzbN2172VR

Spookiest Box Set (3 in 1): Discover America's Most Haunted Destinations (2016)
https://read.amazon.com/kp/embed?asin=B01HH2OM4I&preview=newtab&linkCode=kpe&ref=cm_sw_r_kb_dp_Anz-xbT3SDEZS

MOST HAUNTED and SPOOKIEST Sampler Box Set: Featuring *A GHOST HUNTER'S GUIDE TO THE MOST HAUNTED PLACES IN AMERICA* and *SPOOKIEST CEMETERIES* (2017)
https://read.amazon.com/kp/embed?asin=B01N17EEOM&preview=newtab&linkCode=kpe&ref=cm_sw_r_kb_dp_JFLybCTN3QEF

≈

Terrance Zepke

STOP TALKING SERIES

Stop Talking & Start Writing Your Book (2015)
https://read.amazon.com/kp/embed?asin=B012YHTIAY&preview=newtab&linkCode=kpe&ref_=cm_sw_r_kb_dp_qlrQwb1N7G3YF

Stop Talking & Start Publishing Your Book (2015)
https://read.amazon.com/kp/embed?asin=B013HHV1LE&preview=newtab&linkCode=kpe&ref_=cm_sw_r_kb_dp_WlrQwb1F63MFD

Stop Talking & Start Selling Your Book (2015)
https://read.amazon.com/kp/embed?asin=B015YAO33K&preview=newtab&linkCode=kpe&ref_=cm_sw_r_kb_dp_ZkrQwb188J8BE

Stop Talking & Start Writing Your Book Series (3 in 1) Box Set (2016)
https://www.amazon.com/Stop-Talking-Start-Writing-Box-ebook/dp/B01M58J5AZ/ref=sr_1_5?s=books&ie=UTF8&qid=1475974073&sr=1-5&keywords=stop+talking+and+start+writing

≈

A Ghost Hunter's Guide to the Most Haunted Historic Sites in America

CAROLINAS FOR KIDS SERIES

Lighthouses of the Carolinas for Kids (2009)
http://www.amazon.com/Lighthouses-Carolinas-Kids-Terrance-Zepke/dp/1561644293/ref=asap_bc?ie=UTF8

Pirates of the Carolinas for Kids (2009)
https://read.amazon.com/kp/embed?asin=B01BJ3VSWK&preview=newtab&linkCode=kpe&ref_=cm_sw_r_kb_dp_rGrXwb0XDTSTA

Ghosts of the Carolinas for Kids (2011)
https://read.amazon.com/kp/embed?asin=B01BJ3VSVQ&preview=newtab&linkCode=kpe&ref_=cm_sw_r_kb_dp_XLrXwb0E7N1AK

≈

Terrance Zepke

GHOSTS OF THE CAROLINAS SERIES

Ghosts of the Carolina Coasts (1999)
http://www.amazon.com/Ghosts-Carolina-Coasts-Terrance-Zepke/dp/1561641758/ref=asap_bc?ie=UTF8

The Best Ghost Tales of South Carolina (2004)
http://www.amazon.com/Best-Ghost-Tales-South-Carolina/dp/1561643068/ref=asap_bc?ie=UTF8

Ghosts & Legends of the Carolina Coasts (2005)
https://read.amazon.com/kp/embed?asin=B01AGQJABW&preview=newtab&linkCode=kpe&ref_=cm_sw_r_kb_dp_VKrXwb1Q09794

The Best Ghost Tales of North Carolina (2006)
https://read.amazon.com/kp/embed?asin=B01BJ3VSV6&preview=newtab&linkCode=kpe&ref_=cm_sw_r_kb_dp_6IrXwb0XKT90Q

≈

A Ghost Hunter's Guide to the Most Haunted Historic Sites in America

BOOKS & GUIDES FOR THE CAROLINAS SERIES

Pirates of the Carolinas (2005)
http://www.amazon.com/Pirates-Carolinas-Terrance-Zepke/dp/1561643440/ref=asap_bc?ie=UTF8

Coastal South Carolina: Welcome to the Lowcountry (2006)
http://www.amazon.com/Coastal-South-Carolina-Welcome-Lowcountry/dp/1561643483/ref=asap_bc?ie=UTF8

Coastal North Carolina: Its Enchanting Islands, Towns & Communities (2011)
http://www.amazon.com/Coastal-North-Carolina-Terrance-Zepke/dp/1561645117/ref=asap_bc?ie=UTF8

Lighthouses of the Carolinas: A Short History & Guide (2011)
https://read.amazon.com/kp/embed?asin=B01AGQJA7G&preview=newtab&linkCode=kpe&ref_=cm_sw_r_kb_dp_UHrXwb09A22P1

≈

MORE BOOKS BY TERRANCE ZEPKE

Lowcountry Voodoo: Tales, Spells & Boo Hags (2009)
https://read.amazon.com/kp/embed?asin=B018WAGUC6&preview=newtab&linkCode=kpe&ref=cm_sw_r_kb_dp_UmrQwb19AVSYG

Ghosts of Savannah (2012)
http://www.amazon.com/Ghosts-Savannah-Terrance-Zepke/dp/1561645303/ref=asap_bc?ie=UTF8

How to Train Any Puppy or Dog Using Three Simple Strategies (2017)
https://www.amazon.com/Train-Puppy-Using-Simple-Strategies-ebook/dp/B01MZ5GN2M/ref=asap_bc?ie=UTF8

*Fiction books written under a pseudonym

≈

Message from the Author

The primary purpose of this guide is to introduce you to some titles you may not have known about. Another reason for it is to let you know all the ways you can connect with me. Authors love to hear from readers. We truly appreciate you more than you'll ever know. Please feel free to send me a comment or question via the comment form found on every page on www.terrancezepke.com and www.terrancetalkstravel.com or follow me on your favorite social media. Don't forget that you can also listen to my writing podcast on iTunes, **A Writer's Journey**, or my travel show, **Terrance Talks Travel: Über Adventures** on Blog Talk Radio and iTunes. The best way to make sure you don't miss any episodes of these shows (and find a complete archive of shows), new book releases and giveaways, contests, my TRIP PICK OF THE WEEK, cheap travel tips, free downloadable ghost and travel reports, and more is to subscribe to **Terrance Talks Travel** on www.terrancetalkstravel.com or *Mostly Ghostly* on www.terrancezepke.com. If you'd like to learn more about any of my books, you can find in-depth descriptions and "look inside" options through most online booksellers. Also, please note that links to book previews have been included in SERIES section of this booklet for your convenience.

Thank you for your interest and HAPPY READING!

Terrance

See the next page for a sneak peek of the second book in Terrance Zepke's 'most haunted' series:

A GHOST HUNTER'S GUIDE TO THE MOST HAUNTED HOUSES IN AMERICA

Now available from Safari Publishing

Korner's Folly House

FUN FACTS:

The structure has been dubbed "The Strangest House in the World."

The house has been officially certified as "haunted" by as many as four ghosts.

The first private theater in America was inside this house. The theater, Cupid's Park, still exists.

The History

<u>The Strangest House in the World</u>. That's what it has been called by an architectural magazine, *Preservation*, and the name stuck. It's no wonder it's considered such a strange dwelling. It is a three-story house that has seven levels. The 6,000-square foot Victorian mansion has twenty-two rooms with ceiling heights ranging from six feet to twenty-five feet. There are many unusual murals and artwork in the house, as well as a unique air distribution system. Another unusual feature is the smoking room. Accidental fires posed a serious threat in those days. With that in mind, a fireproof room was built onto the house. This is the only place where smoking was permitted within the house. No two doorways are the same. The same is true for the fifteen fireplaces. There are numerous cubbyholes and trapdoors throughout the odd house.

    The house was the architectural vision of one man, Jule Gilmer Korner. He began building the house in 1878. Two years later, he moved in but continued to make changes to the house for many years. It was built to showcase his interior design business, but later it became a home for his family. He hired a freed slave to run his household. She affectionately became known as 'Aunt Dealy.' She took good care of the house and Jule until he got married in 1886. After that, the job fell to his new wife, Polly Alice Masten Korner. A cottage was built behind the house, and Aunt Dealy moved out of the main house and into this outbuilding.

    Jule and Polly had two children. Child-sized rooms were constructed to accommodate them. Many other changes were made, such as the additions of a ladies sitting room and a library. The top story of the house was made into a children's theatre, Cupid's Park. Puppet shows, plays, and recitals were held here for all the children in town to enjoy. Theatrical productions are still produced here on occasion. There is a huge room underneath the theatre that is called the Reception Room. This is where Jule and Polly did most of their entertaining.

Cupid's Park Theatre (top floor of house)

Because of its odd design and never-ending renovations, a visiting cousin once remarked that "This will surely be Jule Korner's folly." Instead of being offended, Jule was amused. He promptly had a plaque made that read "Korner's Folly" and hung it outside the front door.

Jule Korner died in 1924. Right up to his death he was still working on the house because he never felt that it was finished. Polly died ten years later. The property stayed in the family until the 1970s when it was turned over to the non-profit group, Korner's Folly Foundation.

 **The Hauntings**

Korner's Folly has been investigated by several ghost groups and certified as officially haunted. I have spent the night inside the house, along with an investigative team from the Winston-Salem Paranormal Society. We hunkered down for the night in various rooms, which were reportedly the most haunted areas. These included the Reception Room, Cupid's Park, the ladies sitting room, and one of the bedrooms.

The most haunted area of the house is believed to be the Reception Room, so this is where I chose to be. The psychic and a lead investigator were also in the room with me. The bulk of the monitoring equipment was set up here, so we could see what was going on in other parts of the house. The director of the foundation, Bruce Frankel, had given us a private tour and implicit instructions regarding our overnight stay. One of the rules was not to touch the furniture, so the three of us were seated in folding chairs in the middle of the room. Beside me was the "kissing couch." It has an "S" shape so that the man and woman can sit on opposite sides and face one another to talk or steal a kiss.

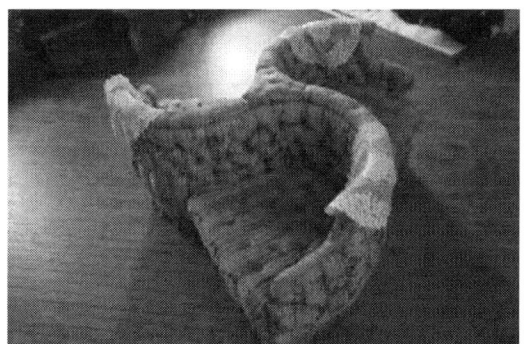

Kissing Couch

At one point in the evening, I suddenly felt very cold and got a weird sensation. As I was trying to figure this out given that it was a hot June night, I felt something on my arm. Startled, I soon realized that it was the hand of the psychic, who was seated next to me. He spoke softly, "I thought you should know that I sense a female presence on the kissing couch." I quickly processed what he was saying. A ghost was beside me!

She moved around the room, standing next to the piano and near the doorway before she disappeared. I knew when she had moved away from me because the cold (and weird) feeling disappeared as suddenly as it had occurred.

We had some questionable EVPs and one of the team members felt a pinch on her behind when no one was standing near her. That was believed to be the spirit of Jule, who had a reputation as a "ladies man" before he got married. He has been known to pinch female visitors on the behind sometimes during their tours.

Another group, Southern Paranormal and Anomaly Research Society (SPARS), certified the house as being "officially haunted" at the conclusion of their investigation. They picked up lots of EVPs of moaning and "peek-a-boo," which was a favorite game of the Korner children. The group also saw unexplainable shadows and orbs on their images.

If all the reports are true, then Korner's Folly is haunted by several spirits. These include Jule Korner, his kids, and Aunt Dealy and Polly Korner.

(Wide angle view of the haunted ballroom and kissing couch)

Visitor Information

The house is open to the public for daytime tours. Also, special events are held throughout the year. The biggest and best is its Holiday Open House. During December, the house is decorated to the hilt, usually by professional interior designers.

413 S. Main Street
Kernersville, NC 27284
www.kornersfolly.org

Kernersville is 2.5 hours from Asheville, NC (155 miles); 7 hours from Columbus, OH (390 miles); and 10.5 hours from Memphis, TN (650 miles).

A Ghost Hunter's Guide to the Most Haunted Historic Sites in America

Index

"Stonewall" Jackson, 74
"The Hole", 54

Abie "Butcher" Maldowitz, 56
Abigail Adams, 39, 40
Abraham Lincoln, 39, 40, 41, 128
Al Capone, 54, 56
Alcatraz, 5, 7, 49, 50, 51, 52, 53, 54, 55, 56, 57, 127
Amazon, 129
American Paranormal Research Association, 55
American Revolution, 61
Andrew Johnson, 40
Anne Surratt, 39
Antonio Lopez de Santa Anna, 31
Appalachian Trail, 74
apparition, 86
Arizona, 3, 5, 88
asylum, 2, 6, 18
Atlanta, 48

Baltimore, 27, 95
Barry Rhodes, 93
Battery Park, 63
Battle of Gettysburg, 24, 25
Battle of Harper's Ferry, 74
Battleship North Carolina, 5, 7, 43, 44, 45, 48
Benjamin Harrison, 37
Bernard Coy, 56
Bette Davis, 121
Birdman of Alcatraz, 50
Blair House, 37
blog, 129
Boston, 21, 68, 106, 112
Bowling Green, 71
Bright Angel Trail, 87
Brown Boys, 83

California, 2, 5, 100, 102, 118, 121, 124
Camp Hill, 75

Capital Area Paranormal Society, 55
Captain Kidd. *See* Captain William Kidd
Captain William Kidd, 62
Cashtown Inn, 26
Cell 14D, 54
cemetery, 18, 32
Charleston, 64
Charlie Grimm, 107
Chicago, 105, 106, 107, 109, 128
Civil War, 2, 18, 23, 24, 37, 51, 53, 68, 73, 74, 77, 114
Coast Guard, 18
cold spots, 41, 107
Colonial Inn, 125
Colonial Williamsburg, 112
Colorado River Basin, 82
Congress, 4, 41, 125, 126
Corpse Rock, 68
Crash Canyon, 85
Crystal Cave, 69
Cuba, 51
Curse of Billy Goat, 7, 108

Dallas, 57
Dangerfield Newby, 77
Danny Bradshaw, 46
David Burns, 41
Davy Crockett, 31, 33, 34, 128
Declaration of Independence, 61
Denver, 88
Devil's Den, 25, 128
Devil's Looking Glass, 69
Doc Barker, 56
Dolley Madison, 39
Dorothy Gish, 121
Dr. John Croghan, 68
Dwight Eisenhower, 37
Eagles Island, 48
East Wing, 37
Eisenhower Executive Office Building, 37
El Tovar Lodge, 85, 88

A Ghost Hunter's Guide to the Most Haunted Historic Sites in America

Eleanor Roosevelt, 39
Ellen Wilson, 39
Ellis Island, 5, 58, 59, 60, 62, 63, 64
Ellis Island Immigrant Hospital, 60
Ellis Island Immigration Museum, 62
EMFs, 33, 47, 107
Empire State Building, 5, 7, 90, 91, 92, 93, 94, 127
England, 68
Evelyn McHale, 92, 128
EVPs, 47, 55, 107, 150
Executive Mansion. *See* White House

Farnsworth House Ghost Walks & Mourning Theater, 28
Farnsworth House Inn, 26
FBI, 52
Federal Bureau of Prisons, 52
Fenway Park, 106
Flint Ridge Baptist Church Cemetery, 69
Florida, 28, 137
Floyd Collins, 69, 70
Floyd Hamilton, 56
Fort Pulaski, 27
France, 31, 61
Fred Harvey, 85
Frederick, 78, 79

General Lee, 24, 74
George "Machine Gun" Kelly, 56
George Washington, 37, 74, 112
Georgia, 2, 3, 23, 27
Gettysburg, 5, 22, 23, 24, 25, 26, 27, 28, 78, 127
Gettysburg College, 25
Gettysburg National Military Park, 23, 25, 27, 78
ghost, 2, 3, 6, 8, 25, 28, 33, 38, 39, 40, 41, 46, 48, 55, 62, 76, 77, 81, 84, 86, 87, 88, 97, 100, 107, 113, 114, 121, 127, 128, 135, 144, 145, 149, 150
Ghost Adventures, 55
Ghost Hunters, 46, 47
Ghost Tours of Harpers Ferry, 78
ghostly sightings, 33, 54
ghosts, 2, 3, 6, 7, 36, 39, 41, 46, 55, 63, 69, 73, 77, 81, 82, 83, 84, 85, 97, 100, 107, 114, 147

Giant's Coffin, 69
Gloria Swanson, 119
Golden Age Passes, 70
Golden Gate Bridge, 5, 7, 50, 96, 97, 98, 99, 100, 101, 102
Golden Gate Pavilion, 98
Golden Gate Recreation Area, 53
Golden Gate Strait, 100
Goodreads, 129
Google Maps, 21
Grace Coolidge, 39
Grand Canyon, 5, 80, 81, 82, 84, 85, 86, 87, 88, 125
Grand Canyon Caverns, 81, 86
Grand Canyon National Park, 81, 82
Grant Wilson, 47
graveyard, 32, 61
Great Earthquake of 1906, 51
Greensboro, 3, 95
Griffith Park, 119, 122

Halfway to Hell Club, 98
Harper's Ferry, 72, 73, 74, 75, 76, 77, 78, 79
Harrisburg, 64
Harry Caray, 107
Hart Island, 5, 7, 9, 16, 17, 18, 19, 20, 21
Haunted North Carolina, 47
High Water Mark of the Rebellion, 24
Hillary Clinton, 41
Historic Hotels of America, 125
Hollywood, 5, 7, 23, 50, 116, 117, 118, 119, 120, 121, 122, 127
Hollywood Cemetery, 23
Hollywood Chamber of Commerce, 118
Hollywood Hills, 119
Hollywood Sign, 5, 7, 116, 117
Hollywoodland. *See* Hollywood
Hopi House, 82, 83, 85
Houston, 34
Hugh Hefner, 119
Humphrey Bogart, 121

Inactive Reserve Fleet, 45

Indianapolis, 42
Iron Horse Restaurant, 77
Island of the Dead. *See* Hart Island

J. Edgar Hoover, 52
James "Tex" Lucas, 56
Jane Vobe, 112
Jason Hawes, 47
Jennie Wade House, 26
Jim Bowie, 31
John "Duke" Wayne, 33
John Adams, 36
John Brown, 73, 74, 75, 76, 77, 78
John Tyler, 39
Joseph Cretzer, 56
Joseph Strauss, 98

Kansas City, 95
King's Arms Tavern, 5, 110, 111, 112, 113, 127
Kolb Skeleton, 87
Korner's Folly House, 147

La Isla de los Alcatraces. *See* Alcatraz
Las Vegas, 57, 88
Laurette Taylor, 121
Liberty Island, 64
Liberty State Park, 63
Life, 92
lighthouse, 51
Long Island Sound, 21
Los Angeles, 57, 118, 121, 123
Louisa Van Slyke, 18

Mammoth Cave, 5, 7, 65, 66, 67, 68, 69, 70, 71, 127
Manhattan, 91, 94
Manuel Fernandez de Castrillon, 33
Mark Nesbitt, 25
Mark Twain, 74
Mary Todd Lincoln, 39
Memphis, 71

Mexico, 31, 51, 66
Milwaukee, 109
Mississippi River, 51, 53
Mummy Ledge, 69

Nancy Reagan, 41
Nashville, 123
National Heritage Area. *See* National Heritage Corridor
National Heritage Corridor, 126
National Heritage Site, 37
National Historic Landmarks, 124
National Historic Site, 126
National Park Service, 25, 37, 54, 57, 63, 76, 82, 124, 125
National Register of Historic Places, 124
National Register of Historic Places., 45, 125, 126
National Trust for Historic Preservation, 125
Native American Indians, 52, 53
Native Americans. *See* Native American Indians
Nevada, 88, 124
New Jersey, 45
New York, 5, 18, 21, 64, 91, 93, 94, 95, 99, 109, 121, 124
New York City, 18, 21, 64, 91, 94, 95, 109
New York Department of Corrections, 18
Newport News, 48
North Carolina, 5, 6, 45, 46, 47, 141, 142
North Rim, 84, 88
NPS. *See* National Park Service

Oakland Bay Bridge, 99
Ohio, 21, 28, 124
Old Guide Cemetery, 68
Orlando, 79
Oval Office, 37, 39

paranormal, 2, 3, 20, 26, 28, 30, 41, 46, 47, 69, 106, 107, 127, 144, 145
paranormal activity, 20, 26, 30, 33, 47, 69, 106, 107, 127
paranormal investigations, 33
parapsychology, 6, 135
Peg Entwistle, 122
Pennsylvania, 5, 24, 25, 26, 42, 124

Pennsylvania College. *See* Gettysburg College
Peter Stephens, 74
Phantom Ranch, 83, 84
Philadelphia, 28, 109
Philippines, 51
Pickett's Charge, 28
Prince Alexis, 68
prison, 18, 50, 51, 52, 53, 54, 55, 57
Puerto Rico, 125

Queen Wilhelmina of the Netherlands, 40

Raleigh, 42, 48, 112, 115
Ralph Waldo Emerson, 68
Rapid City, 101
RDU Ghost Trackers, 47
Rees Griffiths, 84
Reformatory for Misdemeanants, 18
Rhine Research Center, 6
Richard Nixon, 37
Richmond, 23, 42
Rikers Island, 18, 21
Rio Grande, 31
Robert Keith, 121
Robert Wiley, 92
Rose Garden, 39
Roy Larson Raymond, 99
Russia, 68
Ruth Proskauer Smith, 18

Sacramento, 101
Salt Lake City, 88
Sam Houston, 31
San Antonio, 34
San Antonio Missions National Park, 34
San Francisco, 56, 57, 98, 99, 101
San Jose, 101
Santa Fe, 123
séance, 41
séances, 36, 41

Seven Wonders of the Modern World, 91
Showboat. *See* Battleship NC
Soldiers' National Cemetery, 23
South Rim, 83, 84, 87, 88
Spain, 31
Spanish-American War, 51
spirit, 26, 32, 39, 47, 54, 56, 62, 68, 69, 76, 77, 84, 92, 107, 114, 121, 150
Springfield, 71
SS Tennessee
　ghost ship, 100
St. Augustine, 115
St. Peter's Catholic Church, 77
State of Liberty National Monument. *See* Statue of Liberty
Statue of Liberty, 5, 58, 59, 60, 61, 64
Stephan Bishop, 68
Steve Goodman, 107

Tallahassee, 34
TAPS, 47
TB Cabins, 69
TB hospital, 66, 68
TB sanitarium. *See* TB hospital
Teddy Roosevelt, 37
Texas, 5, 30, 31, 34, 124
The Alamo, 7, 29, 30, 33, 34
The Cubs, 105, 106, 108, 109
The Suicide Club, 99
Theodore Roosevelt. *See* Teddy Roosevelt
Thomas Jefferson, 37, 39, 112
Trenton, 64
Tribune Company, 107
tuberculosis, 68, 69

U.S. Army, 33, 53
U.S. Secretary of the Interior, 125
U.S. Virgin Islands, 125
United States Department of the Interior, 125
United States Navy, 18
United States of America, 125
Utah, 88

Virginia, 2, 3, 5, 23, 24, 112, 124
virtual tour, 34

Walter Peck, 86
Wandering Woman, 84
Washington, 42
West Wing, 37, 42
White House, 5, 7, 35, 36, 37, 38, 39, 41, 42, 127
William Henry Harrison, 39
William Travis, 31
William Wrigley, 105
Williamsburg, 112, 113, 114, 115
Willie Lincoln, 41
Wilmington, 3, 45, 48
World War I, 52
World War II, 44, 45
Wrigley Field, 5, 7, 103, 104, 105, 106, 107, 127
WWII, *See* World War II

yellow fever epidemic, 18

Safari Publishing

Made in the USA
Middletown, DE
22 January 2018